Welcome to the 30th anniversary edition of Recommended Hotels & Spas, Great Britain & Ireland.

For three decades we have visited and inspected hotels throughout Great Britain and Ireland. Some hotels have been recommended almost continuously from the first 'Derek Johansens' Guide published in 1982. Their continued inclusion can be attributed to their enduring and absolute belief in placing the needs of their guests first. So look out for the 30th Anniversary roundel at the top of their page entry!

We know from your letters and e-mails that you expect the highest standards of accommodation and service and we have set out to match those expectations by our Recommendations within this Guide for 2012.

You can share your experiences by giving Condé Nast Johansens Gift Vouchers to your friends and family. The vouchers can be redeemed at any of our 2012 Recommendations and make a much valued gift for anniversaries and other special occasions. Purchase them at www.condenastjohansens.com/gift-vouchers.

We are always pleased to receive your comments and feedback. The quickest and easiest way to pass on your views is via "Tell us about your stay" at the foot of each hotel page entry on: www.condenastjohansens.com. Finally, don't forget to mention that you are a Condé Nast Johansens Guide user when making an enquiry or booking. You should receive a very warm welcome when you arrive.

Andrew Warren
Managing Director

L'Instant Champagne, with *Vitalie Taittinger.*

Vitalie Taittinger is an active member of the family Champagne House.

CHAMPAGNE TAITTINGER *Reims*

Champagne for the Independently Minded

Condé Nast Johansens Preferred Champagne Partner

Champagne Taittinger is widely stocked in national retailers such as Majestic Wine Warehouse, Sainsbury's, Tesco, Waitrose, www.everywine.co.uk as well as many independent wine merchants. For further information please contact sole UK agents: Hatch Mansfield on 01344 871800 or Email info@hatch.co.uk

www.taittinger.com

About this Guide

Welcome 1
County Maps 4, 5
Key to Symbols 6
Awards for Excellence 11

Recommendations and Regional Maps:

Channel Islands 12
England 18
Ireland 120
Scotland 132
Wales 142

Mini Listings:

Small Hotels, Inns & Restaurants
– Great Britain & Ireland 2012 151
Historic Houses, Castles & Gardens 2012 157
Hotels & Spas – Europe & The Mediterranean 2012 161
Hotels, Inns, Resorts & Spas –
The Americas, Atlantic, Caribbean & Pacific 2012 168

Indexes 185

To find a hotel by location:

- Use the **county maps** at the front of the Guide to obtain a page number for the area of the country you wish to search.
- Turn to the **indexes** at the back of the book, which start on page 185.
- Alternatively, use the **maps** at the front of each colour coded country section where each hotel is marked.

If you cannot find a suitable hotel you may decide to choose one of the properties within the Condé Nast Johansens Recommended Small Hotels, Inns & Restaurants Guide. These more intimate establishments are listed on pages 151-155.

Once you have made your choice please contact the hotel directly. Rates are per room, including VAT and breakfast (unless stated otherwise) and are correct at the time of going to press but you should always check with the hotel before you make your reservation. **When making a booking please mention Condé Nast Johansens as your source of reference.**

Readers should be aware that by making a reservation with a hotel, either by telephone, e-mail or in writing, they are entering into a legal contract. A hotelier under certain circumstances is entitled to make a charge for accommodation when guests fail to arrive, even if notice of the cancellation is given.

Stoke Park, Buckinghamshire, England – p34

Recommendations can be found plotted on more detailed maps at the front of each colour coded country section

Channel Islands 12
England 18
Ireland 120
Scotland 132
Wales 142

Higland p138

Aberdeenshire p134

Argyll & Bute p135

East Lothian p137

SCOTLAND

N. IRELAND

Mayo p128

Galway p125

Clare p122

IRELAND

Wicklow p130

Kerry p127

Cork p123

ENGLAND

WALES

4

SCOTLAND

IRELAND

IRELAND

ENGLAND

WALES

Northumberland p98

Cumbria p44

Durham p66

North Yorkshire p118

Conwy p144

Denbighshire p145

Cheshire p35

Derbyshire p53

Lincolnshire p78

Gwynedd p146

Staffordshire p101

Rutland p99

Powys p148

Worcestershire p117

Warwickshire p112

Pembrokeshire p147

Herefordshire p77

Bedfordshire p29

Gloucestershire p67

Buckinghamshire p33

Bath & NE Somerset p28

Berkshire p31

London p79

Wiltshire p115

Somerset p100

Hampshire p74

Devon p55

Dorset p61

West Sussex p106

East Sussex p102

Cornwall p36

Channel Islands

Jersey p14

Key to Symbols

🛏 [23] Total number of bedrooms

🌿 The property participates in a minimum of 3 environmentally-friendly practices specified by Condé Nast Johansens

🏠 The property is owner managed

⚷ The property is available for exclusive use

🌳 The property is situated in a quiet location

♿ Wheelchair access – we recommend contacting the property to determine the level of accessibility for wheelchair users

👨‍🍳 The property has a chef-patron (the owner of the property is also the chef at the restaurant)

Ⓜ [23] Maximum capacity for meeting/conference facilities on-site

👧 [8] Children are welcome, with minimum age where applicable

🐕 Dogs are welcome in bedrooms or kennels

🛏 At least 1 bedroom has a four-poster bed

📺 Cable/satellite TV in all bedrooms

🔊 Some or all bedrooms provide an iPod docking station

📞 ISDN/modem point available in all bedrooms

📶 Wireless internet connection available in all rooms

🚬 Smoking is allowed in some bedrooms

🛗 A lift available for guests' use

❄ Air conditioning is available in all bedrooms

🏋 Gym/fitness facilities are available on-site

SPA The property has a dedicated spa with on-site qualified staff and an indoor pool, offering extensive body, beauty and water treatments

🌊 Indoor swimming pool on-site

🌊 Outdoor swimming pool on-site

🎾 Tennis court on-site

🚶 Walking – details of local walking routes, an overnight drying room for clothes and packed lunches can be provided by the property

🎣 Fishing on-site

🎣 Fishing can be arranged nearby

⛳ Golf course on-site

⛳ Golf course is available nearby

🎯 Shooting on-site

🎯 Shooting can be arranged nearby

🐎 Horse riding on-site

🐎 Horse riding can be arranged nearby

🚁 The property has a helicopter landing pad

🔔 The property is licensed for wedding ceremonies

L'OCCITANE
EN PROVENCE

A true story

he scents and traditions of the land of
rovence lie at the heart of L'OCCITANE.
has gained its most precious secrets from this
nique region, where Nature is so beautiful
d flowers have long yielded their benefits.

rom their harvests come natural and authentic
incare products, fragrances and toiletries,
fective and deliciously tempting.

ww.loccitane.com

Condé Nast Johansens

Condé Nast Johansens Ltd, 6-8 Old Bond Street, London W1S 4PH
Tel: +44 (0)20 7499 9080 Fax: +44 (0)20 7152 3565
E-mail: info@johansens.com www.condenastjohansens.com

Hotel Inspectors:	Tim Fay
	John Morison
	Mary O'Neill
	Andrew Warren
Production Manager:	Kevin Bradbrook
Production Editor:	Laura Kerry
Senior Designer:	Rory Little
Marketing Manager:	Adam Crabtree
Digital Marketing Manager:	Gemma James
Copywriters:	Stephanie Cook
	Sasha Creed
	Norman Flack
	Debra O'Sullivan
	Rozanne Paragon
Client Services Director:	Fiona Patrick
PA to Managing Director:	Amelia Priday
Managing Director:	Andrew Warren

Whilst every care has been taken in the compilation of this Guide, the publishers cannot accept responsibility for any inaccuracies or for changes since going to press, or for consequential loss arising from such changes or other inaccuracies, or for any other loss direct or consequential arising in connection with information describing establishments in this publication.

Recommended establishments, if accepted for inclusion, pay an annual subscription to cover the costs of inspection, the distribution and production of copies placed in hotel bedrooms and other services.

No part of this publication may be copied or reproduced, stored in a retrieval system or transmitted, in any form or by any means, electronic, mechanical, photocopy, recording or otherwise, without the prior permission of the publishers.

The publishers request readers not to cut, tear or otherwise mark this Guide. No cuttings may be taken without the written permission of the publishers.

Copyright © 2011 Condé Nast Johansens Ltd.
Condé Nast Johansens Ltd. is part of The Condé Nast Publications Ltd.
ISBN 978-1-903665-57-2
Printed in Scotland by Scotprint, Haddington.
Distributed in the UK and Europe by Portfolio, Brentford (bookstores). In North America by Casemate Publishing, Pennsylvania (bookstores).

Luton Hoo Hotel, Golf & Spa, Bedfordshire, England – p29

WILLIS&GAMBIER
Furniture designed for life

Because life is about choices

The Winners of the Condé Nast Johansens 2011 Awards for Excellence

The Condé Nast Johansens 2011 Awards for Excellence were presented at the Condé Nast Johansens Annual Dinner held at The May Fair hotel, London on 8th November 2010. Awards were given to properties from all over the world that represent the finest standards and best value for money in luxury independent travel. An important source of information for these awards was the feedback provided by guests who completed Condé Nast Johansens Guest Survey Reports.

Please nominate a hotel via its entry page on www.condenastjohansens.com, under "Tell us about your stay."

2011 Winners appearing in this Guide:

Most Excellent Hotel
Hambleton Hall – Rutland, England, p99

Most Excellent London Hotel
41 – London, England, p79

Most Excellent Spa
Lucknam Park Hotel & Spa – Wiltshire, England, p115

Most Outstanding Service
Luton Hoo Hotel, Golf & Spa – Bedfordshire, England, p29

Most Excellent Waterside Hotel
Alexandra Hotel and Restaurant – Dorset, England, p64

Most Excellent City Hotel
Rocpool Reserve and Chez Roux – Highland, Scotland, p139

Most Excellent Family Hotel
The Nare Hotel – Cornwall, England, p37

Most Excellent Restaurant
Gidleigh Park – Devon, England, p56

Most Excellent Country House Hotel
Penmaenuchaf Hall – Gwynedd, Wales, p146

Condé Nast Johansens Readers' Award
Newick Park – East Sussex, England, p105

Champagne Taittinger Wine List Award
Linthwaite House Hotel – Cumbria, England, p51

Newick Park, East Sussex, England – p105

GUERNSEY

La Fontenelle

St Sampson

Saint Peter Port

Richmond

La Planque

HERM ISLAND

ALDERNEY

St Anne

SARK

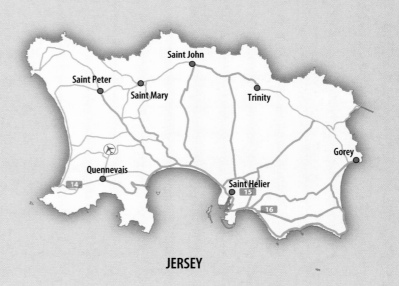

Saint John

Saint Peter

Saint Mary

Trinity

Quennevais

14

Gorey

Saint Helier

15

16

JERSEY

For further information on the Channel Islands, please contact:

Visit Guernsey
Tel: +44 (0)1481 723552
E-mail: enquiries@visitguernsey.com
www.visitguernsey.com

Jersey Tourism
Tel: +44 (0)1534 448800
E-mail: info@jersey.com
www.jersey.com

Sark Tourism
Tel: +44 (0)1481 832345
E-mail: contact@sark.info
www.sark.info

Aurigny Air Services
E-mail: res@aurigny.com
www.aurigny.com

or see **pages 157-160** for details of local historic houses, castles and gardens to visit during your stay.

Longueville Manor, Jersey, Channel Islands – p16

For additional places to stay in the Channel Islands, turn to **pages 151-155** where a listing of our Recommended Hotels & Spas Guide can be found.

The Atlantic Hotel

LE MONT DE LA PULENTE, ST BRELADE, JERSEY, JE3 8HE
Tel: 01534 744101 **International:** +44 (0)1534 744101
Web: www.condenastjohansens.com/atlantic **E-mail:** reservations@theatlantichotel.com

Our inspector loved: The complete experience of superb service, sublime food and ocean sunsets!

Price Guide:
single £100–£150
double £150–£350
suite £350–£550

The Atlantic Hotel is the object of continuous and thoughtful investment by its owner who places the needs of his guests first. Be spoiled by excellent service and admire the contemporary interior decorated with vibrant island art. The Atlantic stands in 6 acres of private grounds alongside La Moye Golf Course with sympathetic cliff-top landscaping that has opened a vista, allowing an uninterrupted view of the ocean across a 5-mile sweep of St Ouen's Bay. Enjoy a special treat and stay in the prestigious Atlantic Suite with its own entrance hall, living room, guest cloakroom and service pantry. Gaining a much deserved Michelin Star, the restaurant showcases modern British cuisine, with an emphasis on seafood and fresh local produce. Be sure to book in advance.

Awards/Recognition: Condé Nast Johansens Most Excellent Waterside Hotel 2010; 1 Star Michelin 2011; 4 AA Rosettes 2011–2012

Location: A13, 0.5 miles; St Helier, 5 miles; Jersey Airport, 3 miles

Attractions: Durrell Wildlife Conservation Trust; Eric Young Orchid Foundation; Jersey War Tunnels; La Mare Vineyards

The Club Hotel & Spa, Bohemia Restaurant

GREEN STREET, ST HELIER, JERSEY JE2 4UH
Tel: 01534 876500 **International:** +44 (0)1534 876500
Web: www.condenastjohansens.com/theclubjersey **E-mail:** reservations@theclubjersey.com

Our inspector loved: *The contemporary style and exceptional dining experience.*

Price Guide:
double/twin from £135
suite from £295

 SPA

Awards/Recognition: 1 Star Michelin 2011; 4 AA Rosettes 2011-2012

Location: A15, 0.25 miles; Jersey Airport, 5 miles

Attractions: Shopping in St Helier; Maritime Museum; Jersey Pottery; Elizabeth Castle and Harbour

The Club Hotel & Spa reflects the real buzz that exudes from St Helier itself. Furnished with contemporary design and understated luxury in mind, bedrooms and suites are decorated to an exceptionally high standard you'll love: LCD TVs, CD players and sleek bathrooms featuring granite surfaces, power showers and all-enveloping sumptuous bathrobes are standard features. The sophisticated Bohemia Restaurant has rapidly gained an enviable reputation with Head Chef Shaun Rankin, participant in BBC2's Great British Menu 2009, at the helm. Private dinner parties up to 24 and a chef's table for six can be accommodated here. Visit the hotel's chic, popular bar, and savour a slower pace of life at the Club Spa by indulging in a treatment. Once refreshed, why not take a walk along the sandy beaches, surf, sail or explore the secret places of this beautiful island.

LONGUEVILLE MANOR

ST SAVIOUR, JERSEY, CHANNEL ISLANDS JE2 7WF
Tel: 01534 725501 **International:** +44 (0)1534 725501
Web: www.condenastjohansens.com/longuevillemanor **E-mail:** info@longuevillemanor.com

Upon arrival at this restored 14th century Norman manor house hotel in St Saviour, you are greeted by delightful staff that know exactly how to blend professionalism with warmth, which is no doubt part of the reason behind the AA Inspectors Choice 5 Star Award. The guest rooms with their welcome of champagne and homemade shortbread are all decorated in warm tones with carefully chosen antiques, beautiful fabrics, digital widescreen TVs and DVD/CD players. Honeymooners are in for a real treat in their secluded suite complete with four-poster bed and hand-painted bath for two. Credited with numerous awards the Oak Room restaurant offers a wonderful atmosphere in which you could spend hours enjoying the fine food and engaging in recommendations from the Master Sommelier. It is also licensed to hold civil wedding ceremonies and with doors opening onto a pretty rose garden this would make a dreamy venue.

Our inspector loved: The contemporary fresh and lighter feel to this iconic hotel.

Price Guide:
single from £175
double/twin £230–£480
suite £500–£800

Awards/Recognition: Relais & Châteaux; 3 AA Rosettes 2011-2012

Location: Just off A3; St Helier, 1.25 miles; Jersey Airport, 7 miles

Attractions: Jersey Pottery; Durrell Wildlife Conservation Trust; Jersey War Tunnels; La Mare Vineyards

A British love affair

We all have a love affair with sleep, yet many of us never truly experience a deep uninterrupted night's sleep, night after night. At Hypnos each Royally Approved bed is individually handmade by master craftsmen using the finest natural materials to guarantee years of sumptuous and rejuvenating slumber. So, to be sure that you have the very best night's sleep, and awake feeling revitalised and refreshed, visit your local Hypnos Retailer and choose a Hypnos bed that's just right for you. Hypnos – the God of Sleep.

Hypnos is proud to be Condé Nast Johansens Preferred Partner for beds and mattresses.

BY APPOINTMENT TO
HER MAJESTY
QUEEN ELIZABETH II
BEDDING AND UPHOLSTERY
MANUFACTURERS

HYPNOS®
THE MOST COMFORTABLE BEDS IN THE WORLD

www.hypnosbeds.com

North West England

SCOTLAND

Berwick-Upon-Tweed

Northumberland National Park

Carlisle

Lake District National Park

Windermere

Kendal

Yorkshire Dales National Park

Isle of Man

Douglas

Barrow-in-Furness

Fleetwood

Blackpool

Preston

Southport

Bolton

Wigan

Manchester

Liverpool

Skip

WALES

North East England

19

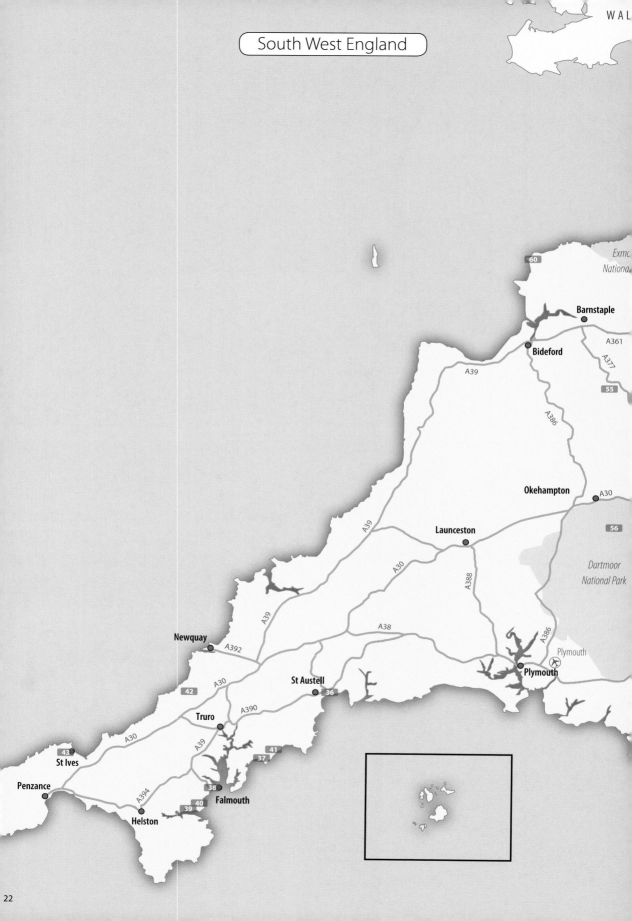

WALES

South West England

Exmoor National Park

Bristol ✈
Bristol
Bath
A4174
A46
A4
A38
A37
A361
A46
A115
A28
Warminster
A36
A350
A39
A303
A350
M5
Taunton
100
A358
A37
A354
A303
Yeovil
A361
A303
Blandford Forum
M5
63
A37
65
Exeter ✈
Exeter
A30
57
Bourn
A377
64
Bridport
A35
Bourne
A30
59
Dorchester
A35
A354
A38
A380
Weymouth
Torquay
A385
Kingsbridge
58

Southern England

Cheltenham

Stow-on-the-Wold

Cirencester

Swindon

Marlborough

Oxford

Newbury

Reading

Basingstoke

Winchester

Southampton

Salisbury

Bournemouth

New Forest

Isle of Wight

Cowes

Portsmouth

Chichester

Bognor Regis

Guildford

Windsor

Heathrow

Aylesbury

Brackley

Milton Keynes

Luton

South East England

London, England

England

For further information on England, please contact:

Cumbria Tourist Board
www.cumbriatourism.org

East of England Tourist Board
Tel: +44 (0)1284 727470
E-mail: info@eet.org.uk
www.visiteastofengland.com

Heart of England Tourism
www.visittheheart.co.uk

Visit London
Tel: 0870 156 6366
www.visitlondon.com

North East England Tourism Team
www.visitnortheastengland.com

North West Tourist Board
www.visitenglandsnorthwest.com

Tourism South East
Tel: +44 (0)23 8062 5400
www.visistsoutheastengland.com

South West Tourism
Tel: 0870 442 0880
E-mail: info@swtourism.org.uk
www.swtourism.co.uk

Welcome to Yorkshire
E-mail: info@yorkshire.com
www.yorkshire.com

English Heritage
Tel: +44 (0)870 333 1181
www.english-heritage.org.uk

Historic Houses Association
Tel: +44 (0)20 7259 5688
E-mail: info@hha.org.uk
www.hha.org.uk

The National Trust
Tel: 0844 800 1895
www.nationaltrust.org.uk

or see **pages 157-160** for details of local historic houses, castles and gardens to visit during your stay.

For additional places to stay in England, turn to **pages 151-155** where a listing of our Recommended Small Hotels, Inns & Restaurants can be found.

Coworth Park, Berkshire, England – p31

DUKES HOTEL

GREAT PULTENEY STREET, BATH, SOMERSET BA2 4DN
Tel: 01225 787960 **International:** +44 (0)1225 787960
Web: www.condenastjohansens.com/dukesbath **E-mail:** info@dukesbath.co.uk

Our inspector loved: *The central location and grand townhouse feel of this beautiful Bath hotel.*

Price Guide:
single £99–£125
double/twin £159–£199
suite £179–£239

Awards/Recognition: 2 AA Rosettes 2011-2012

Location: A36, 0.5 miles; M4 jct 18, 8 miles; Bristol Airport, 15.5 miles; London, 90-min train

Attractions: Roman Baths & Pump Room; Thermae Bath Spa; Theatre Royal; Bath Abbey

Dukes Hotel is a charming and relaxed Grade 1 townhouse hotel, full of character and style. This is evident as soon as you walk through the elegant entrance below half-moon shaped decorative glass, edged by slim, black, wrought-iron railings. Built from Bath stone, the hotel is a former Palladian mansion, and today basks in a sense of understated luxury. Most guest rooms and suites have original intricate plasterwork and large sash windows, and from front rooms you can see more Palladio-inspired façades, while those at the back look out to rolling hills. The 2 AA Rosette awarded Cavendish Restaurant is light, airy and relaxing, and you can enjoy the best organic and free-range British ingredients, including Cornish lamb, local Somerset beef and seafood delivered daily from Devon.

Luton Hoo Hotel, Golf & Spa

THE MANSION HOUSE, LUTON HOO, LUTON, BEDFORDSHIRE LU1 3TQ
Tel: 01582 734437 **International:** +44 (0)1582 734437
Web: www.condenastjohansens.com/lutonhoo **E-mail:** reservations@lutonhoo.co.uk

Our inspector loved: *The excellent service and spa located with in the grounds of this beautiful country house.*

Price Guide:
double/twin £230-£395
suite £495-£895

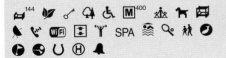

Awards/Recognition: Condé Nast Johansens Most Outstanding Service 2011; 2 AA Rosettes 2011-2012

Location: A1081, 1 mile; M1 jct 10, 3 miles; Luton Airport, 10-min drive; London, 30-min train

Attractions: Central London; Hatfield House and Gardens; Woburn Abbey Safari Park; Knebworth House.

The sweeping drive that leads up to Luton Hoo builds a sense of excitement as you arrive at this impressive grade 1 listed historic mansion. Restored to its original splendour it sits overlooking 1,000 acres of Bedfordshire parkland and formal gardens once designed by Capability Brown. Remarkable care as been taken with the restoration of the stonework and with the soft furnishing of silks, panelling and marquetry. The master bedrooms in the mansion house give a luxurious glimpse of the past. More contemporary bedrooms are to be found in the outbuildings close by; the Parklands and Flower Garden. Take tea in the Italianate drawing room or experience the elegance of the former state dining room, now the Wernher Restaurant. There is plenty to occupy you including the spa, a challenging 18-hole golf course and tennis courts.

MOORE PLACE HOTEL

ASPLEY GUISE VILLAGE, MILTON KEYNES, BEDFORDSHIRE MK17 8DW
Tel: 01908 282000 **International:** +44 (0)1908 282000
Web: www.condenastjohansens.com/mooreplace **E-mail:** manager@mooreplace.com

Our inspector loved: *The newly refurbished rooms with their contemporary styling are a great addition.*

Price Guide:
single £59–£130
double/twin £89–£130
suite £150–£195

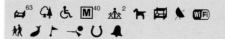

Situated in the village of Aspley Guise just 1.5 miles from the M1, this delightful country house hotel has undergone a sympathetic restoration to suit the original 1786 building. Relax and enjoy the attractive patio courtyard, rock garden and waterfall. 63 comfortably appointed bedrooms offer lots of little extras including a welcoming drink and large toweling bathrobes. 10 bedrooms with individual character are to be found in the converted, listed cottage. The highly acclaimed Greenhouse Restaurant, rated amongst the best in the area, is housed in the Victorian-style conservatory, and serves traditional English menus with a European twist. As well as being perfect for weddings, private dinners, conferences and special occasions, Moore Place is ideally situated for you to explore places of interest nearby.

Location: M1 jct 13, 1.65 miles; Milton Keynes Railway Station, 8 miles; Luton Airport, 19 miles

Attractions: Woburn Abbey; Whipsnade Zoo; Waddesdon Manor; Bletchley Park

COWORTH PARK

BLACKNEST ROAD, ASCOT, BERKSHIRE SL5 7SE
Tel: 01344 876600 **International:** +44 (0)1344 876600
Web: www.condenastjohansens.com/coworthpark **E-mail:** info.coworthpark@dorchestercollection.com

Our inspector loved: *The refreshingly contemporary country house experience with exceptional dining, service and superb spa.*

Price Guide: (room only, excluding VAT)
stable superior £215-£500
mansion superior £275-£575
suites from £335

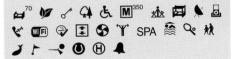

Location: A30, 5 min drive; M3 jct 3, 10 miles; M25 jct 13, 5.5 miles; Gatwick Airport, 45 miles; Heathrow Airport, 20-min drive

Attractions: Windsor Great Park; Legoland; Windsor Castle; Wentworth Golf Course

Coworth Park is a renovated Georgian mansion house that is idyllically set within 240 acres of picturesque parkland on the borders of Windsor Great Park. This very special luxury retreat features a seamless combination of traditional architecture, contemporary interior design, exquisite bespoke furniture and impeccable service – the perfect recipe for a memorable stay. Put your feet up safe in the knowledge that you will be well looked after and take the time to appreciate each of the 3 restaurants' unbridled passion for exceptional cooking. In fact, Coworth Park has appointed one of the UK's most celebrated and talented chefs, John Campbell, to oversee the fine dining restaurant. Each mouth-watering meal is innovative, freshly prepared and impeccably served; undoubtedly some of the best cuisine on offer in the UK today. Golf enthusiasts are also in for a treat with the world-class Wentworth Golf Club located nearby.

THE FRENCH HORN

SONNING-ON-THAMES, BERKSHIRE RG4 6TN
Tel: 01189 692204 **International:** +44 (0)1189 692204
Web: www.condenastjohansens.com/frenchhorn **E-mail:** info@thefrenchhorn.co.uk

Our inspector loved: The warm welcome, excellent service and fine cuisine that make it a joy to return time after time.

Price Guide:
single £125–£170
double/twin £160–£215

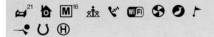

Awards/Recognition: 2 AA Rosettes 2011-2012

Location: A4, 1 mile; M4 jct 10, 3 miles; Reading, 3 miles; Heathrow Airport, 20 miles

Attractions: Henley; Windsor Castle; Stratfield Saye; The Mill Theatre

For over 150 years The French Horn has served as a charming riverside hotel. Today, it continues that fine tradition of comfortable accommodation, excellent service and gourmet food. Choose to stay in bedrooms or suites located in the hotel or within riverside cottages that are ideally suited for longer stays, and make sure to request a riverside view. The old panelled bar provides an intimate scene for pre-dinner drinks in the award-winning restaurant with its speciality of locally reared duck, spit roasted on-site over an open fire. The restaurant is a lovely setting for lunch, while at night, diners can enjoy the floodlit view of the graceful weeping willows which fringe the river. Dinner is served by candlelight and the cuisine is a mixture of French and English cooking that uses the freshest ingredients alongside a fine and extensive wine list. This is the perfect location for a romantic getaway, special celebration or corporate event.

DANESFIELD HOUSE HOTEL AND SPA

HENLEY ROAD, MARLOW-ON-THAMES, BUCKINGHAMSHIRE SL7 2EY
Tel: 01628 891010 **International:** +44 (0)1628 891010
Web: www.condenastjohansens.com/danesfieldhouse **E-mail:** sales@danesfieldhouse.co.uk

Our inspector loved: The panoramic views from the terrace and fine dining experience.

Price Guide:
single from £150
double/twin from £159
suites from £249

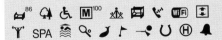

Awards/Recognition: 1 Star Michelin 2011; Condé Nast Johansens Most Excellent Hotel Meeting Venue 2010; Condé Nast Johansens Taittinger Wine List Award, Special Commendation Best Dessert Wine List 2010; 4 AA Rosettes 2011-2012; Voted 13th top restaurant in the UK in Good Food Guide 2011

Location: A4155, 0.2 miles; M40 jct 4, 7 miles; Marlow, 3 miles; Heathrow airport, 23 miles

Attractions: Henley; Windsor; Ascot; River Walks

Built at the end of the 19th century in an imposing Victorian style, Danesfield House Hotel and Spa is set within 65 acres of stunning gardens overlooking the River Thames with panoramic views across the Chilterns. The executive bedrooms are richly decorated and furnished. Guests may relax in the magnificent Grand Hall, with its minstrels' gallery, in the sun-lit atrium or comfortable bar before taking dinner in one of the 2 restaurants. The Michelin starred restaurant, Adam Simmonds at Danesfield House features the delicious cuisine of chef Adam Simmonds and The Orangery which offers a more traditional menu. Leisure facilities include the award-winning spa with 20-metre ozone-cleansed pool, sauna, steam room, gymnasium and superb treatment rooms. There are also 10 private banqueting and conference rooms. When in London visit Danesfield's award winning sister spa, Spa Illuminata in Mayfair.

STOKE PARK

PARK ROAD, STOKE POGES, BUCKINGHAMSHIRE SL2 4PG
Tel: 01753 717171 **International:** +44 (0)1753 717171
Web: www.condenastjohansens.com/stokepark **E-mail:** info@stokepark.com

Our inspector loved: The choice of traditional of contemporary styled rooms, the great spa, excellent cuisine and beautiful location offer something for every occasion.

Price Guide: (a selection of indulgence breaks are often available)
superior £265
deluxe £315
executive £365
junior suite £495
executive suite £675

Stoke Park hotel and golf resort offers 5 AA star luxury accommodation set amidst 350 acres of parkland. For over 900 years it has been at the heart of English heritage, playing host to royalty and aristocracy. The magnificence of the Palladian mansion is echoed in the beautiful interior, enhanced by exquisite antiques, fabrics and paintings. Overlooking breathtaking views, the 49 rooms and suites certainly live up to expectations. All individually furnished, 21 of the bedrooms mirror the hotel's period style, whilst above the £20-million health pavilion, the other 28 resonate luxury modern design. Private bars, cosy lounges, 8 function rooms and the finest restaurants outside London are perfect for entertaining and events. Since 1908 the hotel has been home to one of the world's finest 27-hole championship golf courses. This, along with the spa and health pavilion, truly confirms the hotel's position as one of the country's leading hotel-spa resorts.

Awards/Recognition: 2 AA Rosettes 2011-2012

Location: Off the B416; M4 jct 6, 4.5 miles; Windsor, 5 miles; Heathrow Airport, 7 miles

Attractions: Windsor Castle; Ascot; Henley; Legoland

THE MERE GOLF RESORT & SPA

CHESTER ROAD, MERE, KNUTSFORD, CHESHIRE WA16 6LJ
Tel: 01565 830155 **International:** +44 (0)1565 830155
Web: www.condenastjohansens.com/themereresort **E-mail:** sales@themereresort.co.uk

Our inspector loved: *Being pampered in the new spa after a round of golf on the outstanding course.*

Price Guide:
single from £110
double £120-£200
suite £240-£420

Location: A556, 250yds; M6 jct 19, 2 miles; M56 jct 7, 3 miles; Mancherster International Airport, 9.5 miles

Attractions: Liverpool; Tatton Park; Arley Hall & Gardens; Trafford Centre

The Mere has provided a stunning venue for weddings and corporate events for the past 25 years, and in March 2012 it will combine its superb championship golf course and world-class spa with the opening of its new luxury hotel accommodation. Deep in the heart of the Cheshire countryside, the 81 bedrooms and suites will fully complement the superior leisure facilities. Created out of 150 acres of parkland, the 18-hole golf course is as beautiful as it is challenging, providing the perfect environment for a day's play and networking, or a relaxing round. The resort's lakeside setting is wonderfully romantic for a wedding and experienced co-ordinators will rise to the occasion and take care of the entire day from civil ceremonies to evening banquets and intimate receptions. Whether you're staying for business or pleasure the Health Club & Spa is a must with its state-of-the-art equipment, refined contemporary spa pool and indulgent treatments.

CARLYON BAY HOTEL, SPA & GOLF RESORT

SEA ROAD, ST AUSTELL, CORNWALL PL25 3RD
Tel: 01726 812304 **International:** +44 (0)1726 812304
Web: www.condenastjohansens.com/carlyonbay **E-mail:** reservations@carlyonbay.com

Our inspector loved: The fabulous location, attentive service and the hotels own private beach.

Price Guide: (room only)
single £95-£130
double £145-£270
state room £280-£310

Awards/Recognition: 1 AA Rosette 2010-2011

Location: A391, 2 Miles; St Austell, 3 miles; A30, 13 miles; Newquay Airport, 18 miles

Attractions: The Eden Project; Lost Gardens of Heligan; The Minack Theatre; Fowey

Whether visiting Cornwall on a well-deserved family break or dreaming of a few rounds on a stunning championship golf course, this charming hotel, with its warm Cornish hospitality and truly inspiring location, will certainly exceed all your expectations. From its spectacular vantage point above the cliffs of St Austell Bay featuring idyllic private beaches, take advantage of all the leisure facilities the hotel has to offer, including a heated swimming pool. Alternatively, simply languish in the luxurious spa - a decadent way to spend the day! The bedrooms have panoramic views of the coastline and are beautifully decorated to imbue a sense of well-being and comfort. In addition, there is a wide choice of dishes at the restaurant. So relax and let your hosts take care of everything!

THE NARE HOTEL

CARNE BEACH, VERYAN-IN-ROSELAND, TRURO, CORNWALL TR2 5PF
Tel: 01872 501111 **International:** +44 (0)1872 501111
Web: www.condenastjohansens.com/nare **E-mail:** stay@narehotel.co.uk

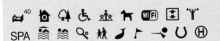

Our inspector loved: *The beautiful beach front location, excellent service and cuisine.*

Price Guide:
single £136-£260
double/twin £262-£488
suite £324-£746

SPA

Awards/Recognition: Condé Nast Johansens Most Excellent Family Hotel 2011; 2 AA Rosette 2011-2012

Location: St Mawes, 8 miles, Truro, 12 miles; St Austell, 12 miles ; A30, 15 miles

Attractions: Eden Project; Lost Gardens of Heligan; Cornish Gardens; National Maritime Museum Falmouth

This absolute gem of a 4 star hotel is superbly positioned overlooking the fine sandy beach of Gerrans Bay. Thanks to Toby Ashworth's proprietorial presence, the hotel has carefully evolved over the years and is considered the most comfortable Cornwall hotel. The winner of Condé Nast Johansens Most Excellent Family Hotel 2011, most bedrooms look out to the sea and have patios and balconies with spectacular views. More sea views are enjoyed from the hotel's 2 restaurants. The main dining room offers a traditional dining experience off the table d'hôte menus where classic English cuisine features local seafood dishes such as Portloe lobster and crab and delicious home-made puddings with generous helpings of Cornish cream. Dinner is also always available in the more informal Quarterdeck Restaurant where al fresco lunches may be taken on the terrace. Explore the glorious Roseland Peninsula's coastline and villages, not forgetting Cornwall's houses and gardens.

St Michael's Hotel & Spa

GYLLYNGVASE BEACH, FALMOUTH, CORNWALL TR11 4NB
Tel: 01326 312707 **International:** +44 (0)1326 312707
Web: www.condenastjohansens.com/stmichaelsfalmouth **E-mail:** info@stmichaelshotel.co.uk

Our inspector loved: The beautiful new restaurant, bar and lounge area make St Michael's even more welcoming than ever.

Price Guide: (per person)
double/twin £59–£105
suite £105–£155

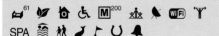

SPA

St Michael's Hotel & Spa, Cornwall, has been carefully and extensively refurbished, resulting in a state-of-the-art health club, spa, award-winning restaurant, and contemporary bedrooms, bars and conference suites. The Flying Fish Restaurant, overlooking the sea and gardens, changes menus regularly so you can sample Cornwall's best fresh fish, seafood and seasonal produce. The sun terrace is the perfect spot for alfresco dining. Surrounded by sub-tropical gardens, the Spa offers an impressive range of health and relaxation treatments, and you can also take a dip in the indoor pool and work out in the large fitness suite. The hotel is ideally located for all the attractions of Falmouth and the nearby area: feel the sand between your toes on the blue flag beach, directly opposite the hotel, or visit the Eden Project within an hour's drive.

Location: Just off A39; Truro, 11.7 miles; Newquay Airport, 25 miles

Attractions: National Maritime Museum; Land's End; Eden Project; Coastal walks

BUDOCK VEAN - THE HOTEL ON THE RIVER

NEAR HELFORD PASSAGE, MAWNAN SMITH, FALMOUTH, CORNWALL TR11 5LG
Tel: 01326 252100 **International:** +44 (0)1326 252100
Web: www.condenastjohansens.com/budockvean **E-mail:** relax@budockvean.co.uk

Our inspector loved: *The excellent service and facilities and beautiful grounds.*

Price Guide: (including dinner)
single £72–£140
double/twin £144–£280
suite £240–£350

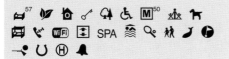

Awards/Recognition: 1 AA Rosette 2011–2012

Location: M5 jct 30, 100 miles; A39, 12 miles; Falmouth, 6 miles; Newquay Airport, 30 miles

Attractions: Trebah Gardens; Glendurgan Gardens; National Maritime Museum Falmouth; Eden Project

This family run 4 star hotel is set in 65 acres of outstanding natural beauty with award-winning gardens and a private foreshore on the Helford River. One of the country's finest green hotels, Budock Vean is all about relaxation and pampering and has become a destination in itself, recommended by Condé Nast Johansens since 1983 and current recipient of the Green Tourism Business Scheme Gold Award. Guests can enjoy a large indoor pool, outdoor hot tub, sauna, tennis courts, a snooker room, boating, fishing, a Natural Health Spa plus unlimited use of the 9-hole golf course which was originally designed by James Braid of St Andrews fame. A local ferry will take you from the hotel's jetty to waterside pubs and you can even enjoy a trip on the hotel's own river boat. Imaginative dinners specialise in fresh seafood, which can be walked off on a magnificent myriad of local country and coastal walks.

MEUDON HOTEL

MAWNAN SMITH, NEAR FALMOUTH, CORNWALL TR11 5HT
Tel: 01326 250541 **International:** +44 (0)1326 250541
Web: www.condenastjohansens.com/meudon **E-mail:** wecare@meudon.co.uk

Our inspector loved: The beautiful gardens and comfortable atmosphere at this classic hotel.

Price Guide: (including dinner)
single £150
double/twin £300
suite £400

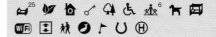

The Pilgrims are fifth generation hoteliers and it shows in the attention, care and enthusiasm they put into running their country house hotel, a haven of peace and beauty where the grounds run down to the sea. The French name of the property originates from a nearby farmhouse built by Napoleonic prisoners of war and called after their longed-for home village. Comfortable bedrooms enjoy spectacular views over the hotel's sub-tropical gardens which tend to be coaxed into early bloom by the Gulf Stream and mild Cornish climate. Local fishermen and farmers supply the kitchen with ingredients to allow a changing seasonal menu. There are endless places to visit and pursuits to indulge in, you can play golf (free in high season) at nearby Falmouth Golf Club, hike the coastal paths or just laze on the private beach.

Location: A39, 5 miles; Falmouth, 4 miles; A30, 13 miles; Newquay Airport NQY, 32 miles

Attractions: National Maritime Museum Falmouth; Trebah Gardens; Pendennis Castle; Eden Project

THE LUGGER HOTEL

PORTLOE, NEAR TRURO, CORNWALL TR2 5RD
Tel: 0844 414 6550 **International:** +44 (0)844 414 6550
Web: www.condenastjohansens.com/lugger **E-mail:** reservations.lugger@ohiml.com

Our inspector loved: The idyllic location, great food and friendly service.

Price Guide: (including dinner)
single from £150
classic from £170
deluxe from £190
superior from £210
cottage suite from £250

Awards/Recognition: 1 AA Rosette 2011–2012

Location: A3078, 2.5 miles; A30, 65 miles; M5 jct 31, 87 miles; Newquay Airport, 29 miles

Attractions: Lost Gardens of Heligan; Pendower and Carne Beaches; Truro; Eden Project

Coastal walks, seafood and luxurious accommodation are all available at this beautiful place that is almost too good to be true. The Lugger is a little gem tucked away in a cove and tiny harbour where you can watch lobster and crab pots being landed and taken away. Its history is an intriguing mix of a 17th-century inn, boat builder's shed and fishermen's cottages. Now transformed into a warm, welcoming hotel, complete with a spa. Rooms are delightful and whilst varying in size have immense character and come stocked with huge bath sheets. You won't be surprised to find out that the menus are heavy on fresh produce such as locally caught seafood, and in the summer you can easily spend hours over lunch and drinks on the sunny terraces admiring the gorgeous, rugged coastline.

Rose-In-Vale Country House Hotel

MITHIAN, ST AGNES, CORNWALL TR5 0QD
Tel: 01872 552202 **International:** +44 (0)1872 552202
Web: www.condenastjohansens.com/roseinvalecountryhouse **E-mail:** reception@rose-in-vale-hotel.co.uk

Our inspector loved: *The peaceful location and comfortable rooms.*

Price Guide:
single from £80
double/twin from £135
suite £260

Awards/Recognition: 1 AA Rosette 2011-2012

Location: A3075, 1.4 miles; A30, 2.3 miles; Newquay Airport, 15 miles

Attractions: Local Beaches; Eden Project; Lost Gardens of Heligan; Various National Trust Gardens

A few miles inland from St Agnes you descend into a tranquil wooded valley and find The Rose-in-Vale, a welcoming Cornish country house hotel surrounded by charming grounds on this private estate. The owners, James and Sara Evans, are extremely hospitable and there is a genuine desire to ensure that you have all you need. A light and very spacious dining room is the setting for the carefully thought-out, seasonal menu which features an impressive 'surf & turf' option letting you enjoy the best of local meat and freshly caught seafood. The Rose-in-Vale provides comfortable bedrooms throughout this picturesque Georgian house including The Rose Suite, which comes with a four-poster bed and the indulgence of a double Jacuzzi bath and a double twelve-jet walk in shower! Outside, you can relax by the swimming pool, in the hot tub, take your dog for a garden walk or simply find a quite corner by the duck pond.

St Ives Harbour Hotel - Porthminster

THE TERRACE, ST IVES, CORNWALL TR26 2BN
Tel: 01736 795221 **International:** +44 (0)1736 795221
Web: www.condenastjohansens.com/stivesharbour **E-mail:** stives@harbourhotels.co.uk

Our inspector loved: The beautiful contemporary interiors that have brought this Victorian hotel back to its former glory.

Price Guide: (per person)
double £62.50-£87.50
suite £125-£150

Location: A3074, 1 mile; A30, 6 miles; Newquay Airport, 27 miles

Attractions: The Tate St Ives; Barbara Hepworth Museum and Gardens; St Michael's Mount; Eden Project

Colourful stone cottages tumbling over each other in narrow, twisting streets, together with stunning sea views and an unspoiled fishing harbour, attracted first artists and then tourists to this picture-perfect part of Cornwall. Overlooking all from on high is St Ives Harbour Hotel - Porthminster, a long, tall, majestic, late 19th-century hotel famed for all-year-round sea side family holidays, romantic honeymoons, luxury spa packages and fine dining. A much loved, stylish hotel looking down to Porthminster Bay, its interior is refreshing and some guest rooms have balconies on which to relax with a morning coffee or afternoon tea. Service cannot be bettered and the award winning cuisine makes optimum use of the abundance of the finest produce from the local surroundings.

FARLAM HALL HOTEL

BRAMPTON, CUMBRIA CA8 2NG
Tel: 016977 46234 **International:** +44 (0)16977 46234
Web: www.condenastjohansens.com/farlamhall **E-mail:** farlam@farlamhall.co.uk

Our inspector loved: *The hospitality at this luxurious and elegant family run borders hotel.*

Price Guide: (including dinner)
single £160–£190
double/twin £300–£360

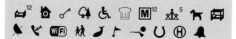

Awards/Recognition: Relais & Châteaux; 2 AA Rosette 2011-2012

Location: A689, 500yds; Brampton, 2.5 miles; M6 jct 43 or 44, 10 miles; Carlisle, 12 miles

Attractions: Hadrians Wall & the Border Country; Lanercost Priory; Carlisle

Picturesque Farlam Hall was opened in 1975 by the Quinion family who over the years have achieved a consistently high standard with their food, service and comfort. Close to championship golf and Hadrian's Wall Heritage Site, this old border house, dating in parts from the 17th century, is set in mature gardens, which can be seen from the elegant lounges and dining room, creating a relaxed and pleasing environment. The fine silver and crystal in the dining room complement the quality of the English country house cooking produced by Barry Quinion and his team of chefs. There are 12 individually decorated bedrooms varying in size and shape, some having Jacuzzi baths, one an antique four-poster bed and there are 2 ground floor bedrooms. Winter and spring breaks are available but the hall is closed for Christmas. An AA 3 Red Stars and Inspectors Choice Hotel.

NETHERWOOD HOTEL

LINDALE ROAD, GRANGE-OVER-SANDS, CUMBRIA LA11 6ET
Tel: 015395 32552 **International:** +44 (0)15395 32552
Web: www.condenastjohansens.com/netherwood **E-mail:** enquiries@netherwood-hotel.co.uk

Our inspector loved: This majestic family-run hotel with lovely views of Morecambe Bay.

Price Guide:
single £60-£120
double £95-£200

Location: B5277, 500 yards; A590, 3 miles; M6 jct 36, 10 miles; Lake Windermere, 5 miles

Attractions: Morecambe Bay; Holker & Levens Hall; Lake District National Park; Leighton Moss RSPB Reserve

Dramatic and stately in appearance, this friendly hotel - overlooking the wonderful Morecombe Bay - was built as a family house in the 19th century and still exudes a warm, family atmosphere thanks to its longstanding owners, the Fallowfields. Impressive oak panelling is a key feature and provides a fitting backdrop to roaring log fires in the public areas. Bedrooms come with views of the sea, woodlands and gardens. In addition to the main house, Rock House has 4 contemporary bedrooms and The Turrets is a castellated executive self-catering cottage with 2 bedrooms and 2 lounges, ideal for families and groups up to 8. Both are situated a short walking distance within the grounds of Netherwood. The restaurant presents local produce and is set on the first floor, which maximises the views over Morecambe Bay. For relaxation there is an indoor pool, spa bath, steam room and fitness centre, and a wide range of treatments are available at Equilibrium, the hotel's health spa.

ARMATHWAITE HALL COUNTRY HOUSE HOTEL AND SPA

BASSENTHWAITE LAKE, KESWICK, CUMBRIA CA12 4RE
Tel: 017687 76551 **International:** +44 (0)17687 76551
Web: www.condenastjohansens.com/armathwaite **E-mail:** reservations@armathwaite-hall.com

Our inspector loved: Enjoying the lovely views from the large outdoor hot tub.

Price Guide:
single £155
double/twin £260–£330
studio suite £370

Awards/Recognition: 1 AA Rosette 2011-2012

Location: A591, 0.25 miles; A66, 1 mile; M6 jct 40, 25 miles; Keswick, 7 miles

Attractions: Trotters World of Animals; Bassenthwaite Lake; Lake District National Park; Wordsworth and Beatrix Potter Museums

This luxurious hotel in the heart of England's Lake District is set within 400 secluded acres of deer park and woodland. Originally a stately home, its facilities and location are impressive; the perfect place for discovering the nearby Bassenthwaite Lake and Skiddaw Mountain. Full of individuality and character, guest rooms range from the most indulgent Studio Suites to Superior and Club rooms. Accommodation set within the main house is more traditional in style while the Spa Wing rooms reflect a contemporary feel. Comfort and relaxation are at the heart of Armathwaite, and the award-winning spa featuring an infinity-edge pool, aroma room, exercise classes and treatment rooms, offers an experience or treatment to suit your needs and lifestyle. In addition, the AA Rosette awarded cuisine, prepared by Master Chef Kevin Dowling, takes full advantage of local seasonal produce and Cumbrian specialities to create inspired English and classical French dishes.

THE LODORE FALLS HOTEL

BORROWDALE, KESWICK, CUMBRIA CA12 5UX
Tel: 017687 77285 **International:** +44 (0)17687 77285
Web: www.condenastjohansens.com/lodorefalls **E-mail:** lodorefalls@lakedistricthotels.net

Our inspector loved: *The outdoor swimming pool with its views over to Derwentwater, and the hot tub beside the river.*

Price Guide:
single £92–£149
double £156–£289
suite £290–£458

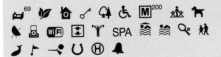

Location: B5289, 10yds; A66, 4 miles; M6 jct 40, 22 miles; Keswick, 3.5 miles

Attractions: Derwentwater Launch; Keswick Golf Club; Trotters World of Animals; Honistor Slate Mine with new Via Ferrata walk/climb

Close your eyes and imagine stunning lake and mountain views, a waterfall in landscaped gardens, warm hospitality, beauty treatments and an array of leisure facilities as well as good food and service. Open your eyes and see The Lodore Falls, a 4-star hotel in the picturesque Borrowdale Valley. The 69 en-suite Fell Side and Lake View rooms include family rooms and luxurious suites, some with balconies. Light meals and coffee can be enjoyed in the comfortable lounges, whilst the cocktail bar is the ideal venue for a pre-dinner drink. The Lake View restaurant serves the best in English and Continental cuisine accompanied by fine wines. The Beauty Salon, with its 4 beautiful treatment rooms, use the famous Elemis beauty products in its treatments and offers pamper days, luxury days and a very special Waterfall Treatment Day. Family activity inclusive holidays are available.

DALE HEAD HALL LAKESIDE HOTEL

THIRLMERE, KESWICK, CUMBRIA CA12 4TN
Tel: 017687 72478 **International:** +44 (0)17687 72478
Web: www.condenastjohansens.com/daleheadhall **E-mail:** onthelakeside@daleheadhall.co.uk

Our inspector loved: The beautiful and peaceful location. This is the only house on Lake Thirlmere.

Price Guide: (including dinner)
single £130–£160
double £210–£330

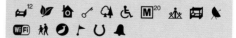

Awards/Recognition: 1 AA Rosettes 2011-2012

Location: A591, 0.25 miles; M6 jct 40, 14 miles; Keswick, 4 miles; Windermere, 14 miles

Attractions: Dove Cottage and The Wordsworth Museum; Honister Slate Mine; Theatre by the Lake; Rookin House Farm Activity Centre

The key handed to you upon arrival at Dale Head Hall isn't simply the key to a room – it's the key to complete relaxation. This is the boast of the Hill family, caring owners of this fine hotel that stands alone on the shores of Lake Thirlmere. A bird-watcher's paradise, the setting is nothing less than idyllic, and inside, the furnishings and atmosphere are warm and welcoming. Some of the rooms are located in the Elizabethan house, while others are in the Victorian extension; some have stunning lake views as does the lounge, or mountain views. You can enjoy superb food prepared from the finest, freshest seasonal local produce alongside an extensive international wine list, in the award-winning lakeside restaurant.

GILPIN HOTEL & LAKE HOUSE

CROOK ROAD, WINDERMERE, CUMBRIA LA23 3NE
Tel: 015394 88818 **International:** +44 (0)15394 88818
Web: www.condenastjohansens.com/gilpinlodge **E-mail:** hotel@gilpinlodge.co.uk

Our inspector loved: The new luxurious suites in the Lake House with their exclusive pool, spa and private lake.

Price Guide: (based on 2 sharing, including 5-course dinner)
single £200-£540
double/twin £310–£400
garden suite £440
lake house suite £490-£580

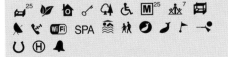

Awards/Recognition: Relais & Châteaux; 3 AA Rosettes 2011-2012

Location: B5284, 200yds; A591, 6 miles; M6 jct 36, 12 miles; Windermere, 2 miles

Attractions: Windermere; Beatrix Potter Museum; Holker & Levens Halls; Blackwell Arts and Crafts House

A luxury Lake District Hotel, Gilpin Hotel has been family run for over 21 years, and as well as having won a multitude of awards it is well loved by those who visit for special breaks, a romantic weekend or simply as a haven to unwind. The service is warm and personal yet relaxed, and every room is designed and furnished with huge attention to detail. Many have patio doors leading out onto the beautiful gardens, with spa baths or hot tubs, and in 2010 the family was proud to present the opening of the Gilpin Lake House. Simply stunning, it is located one mile from the Hotel and set in 100 acres of grounds on the shore of a private lake - known as Knipe Tarn - with boat house and jetty, and a spa for exclusive use of Lake House guests. All of the individually created suites make the most of their beautiful setting, and each evening a chauffeur will take you to and from the Hotel's AA 3 Rosette-awarded restaurant for dinner.

HOLBECK GHYLL COUNTRY HOUSE HOTEL

HOLBECK LANE, WINDERMERE, CUMBRIA LA23 1LU
Tel: 01539 432 375 **International:** +44 (0)1539 432 375
Web: www.condenastjohansens.com/holbeckghyll **E-mail:** stay@holbeckghyll.com

Our inspector loved: *The delicious dinner in the oak-panelled restaurant with panoramic views over Lake Windermere.*

Price Guide: (including 4-course dinner)
single from £184
double/twin £245–£430
suite £315–£570

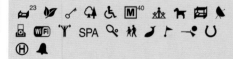

Awards/Recognition: 1 Star Michelin 2011; 3 AA Rosettes 2011-2012

Location: A591, 0.5 mile; M6 jct 36, 20 miles; Windermere, 3 miles; Ambleside, 1 mile

Attractions: Lake Windermere; Lake District National Park; Dove Cottage & Rydal Mount; Brockhole Visitors Centre

Boasting breathtaking views over Lake Windermere and the Lakeland Fells, Holbeck Ghyll is nestled amidst acres of natural beauty. Built in the 19th century, the traditional Arts & Crafts style remains to this day, apparent in the wealth of detail throughout the house including stained-glass windows and carved wooden panelling. Renowned for its restaurant's fine cuisine, which has held a Michelin Star for 11 consecutive years and presents an award-winning wine list, the hotel also offers luxurious accommodation, a health spa and superb service, which includes a concierge facility that can arrange activities from helicopter flights to super car hire. In addition, there is a variety of accommodation to choose from such as deluxe en-suite rooms in the main house, contemporary lodge rooms within the grounds, the exclusive Miss Potter Suite, ideal for special celebrations, and self-contained cottages with private garden and hot tub.

LINTHWAITE HOUSE HOTEL

CROOK ROAD, WINDERMERE, CUMBRIA LA23 3JA
Tel: 015394 88600 **International:** +44 (0)15394 88600
Web: www.condenastjohansens.com/linthwaitehouse **E-mail:** stay@linthwaite.com

Our inspector loved: The unstuffy and friendly ambience of this elegant hotel overlooking Lake Windermere.

Price Guide:
single £171-£244
double £204-£344
suite £283-£554

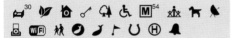

Awards/Recognition: Condé Nast Johansens and Champagne Taittinger Wine List Awards, Wine List of the Year 2011

Location: B5284, 0.25 miles; Windermere, 2 miles; A591, 2 miles; M6 Jct 36, 14 miles

Attractions: Windermere; Beatrix Potter Museums & Dove Cottage; Lake District National Park

Linthwaite House is located at the heart of England within the Lake District, amidst 14 acres of garden and woodland overlooking Lake Windermere and Belle Isle. The hotel combines stylish originality and luxury accommodation with the best of traditional hospitality. Most bedrooms have lake, garden or fell views. Linthwaite's newest room is the luxurious Luxury Lake View room with outdoor 'Hot Tub'. The restaurant offers excellent cuisine with the best of fresh, local produce accompanied by a fine selection of wines. There is a 9 hole putting green within the grounds and a par 3 practice hole. You can if you wish, fish for brown trout in the hotel tarn. Fell walks begin at the front door, and you can follow in the footsteps of Wordsworth and Beatrix Potter to explore the spectacular scenery.

LAKESIDE HOTEL ON LAKE WINDERMERE

LAKESIDE, NEWBY BRIDGE, CUMBRIA LA12 8AT
Tel: 015395 30001 **International:** +44 (0)15395 30001
Web: www.condenastjohansens.com/lakeside **E-mail:** sales@Lakesidehotel.co.uk

Our inspector loved: Watching the ducks being fed while enjoying morning coffee in the Lakeside Conservatory.

Price Guide:
single from £140
double/twin £165–£340
suite from £280

A picturesque and unique location on the edge of Lake Windermere, this classic, relaxed and traditional 4-star hotel will have cast its spell on you by the time your visit is over. Many bedrooms have breathtaking lake vistas, and menus in both the award-winning Lakeview Restaurant or Ruskin's Brasserie include Cumbrian favourites. To get a real Lake's experience there are cruisers berthed adjacent to the hotel ready for further exploration and adventure. For inclement weather the Pool and Spa, exclusively available for hotel residents, comprises of a 17m indoor pool, gym, sauna, steam room and Aveda treatment rooms. For business guests, the new and exclusive Business and Events Centre, Windermere Suite, is located opposite the hotel. Available for exclusive use, it offers delegates the best of both worlds: discreet privacy and 4-star hotel splendour.

Awards/Recognition: Condé Nast Johanens Most Excellent Waterside Hotel Award 2009; 2 AA Rosettes 2011-2012

Location: A590, 1 mile; M6 jct 36, 15 miles; Newby Bridge, 1 mile

Attractions: Windermere Lake Cruisers & Aquarium of the Lakes; Lakeland Motor Museum; Lakeside and Haverthwaite Steam Railway; Holker Hall and Gardens

FISCHER'S BASLOW HALL

CALVER ROAD, BASLOW, DERBYSHIRE DE45 1RR
Tel: 01246 583259 **International:** +44 (0)1246 583259
Web: www.condenastjohansens.com/fischers **E-mail:** reservations@fischers-baslowhall.co.uk

Our inspector loved: The lovingly tended flower and kitchen gardens where the hotel's chefs collect fruit, vegetables and herbs for use in their dishes.

Price Guide:
single £105-£150
double/twin £155–£240

Awards/Recognition: 1 Star Michelin 2011; 4 AA Rosettes 2010–2011

Location: A626, 50yds; Bakewell, 4 miles; M1 Jct 29, 40-min drive; Manchester Airport, 1-hour drive

Attractions: Chatsworth; Haddon Hall; Buxton (Market Town); Peak District National Park

Within walking distance of the Chatsworth Estate, this is the perfect base for exploring the Peak District. Reached via a tree-lined drive, Baslow Hall has all the glorious trademarks of a 17th-century manor house, however the Hall was built in 1907 and remains a beloved family home. Owners Max and Susan Fischer bought the property in 1988 and filled it with their own furniture and art collection to create a personal feel. 11 bedrooms are individually styled with the emphasis on comfort; 6 traditional rooms are located in the Main House and 5 more contemporarily designed rooms are situated in the adjacent Garden Rooms. Food is an important part of Baslow Hall, with Head Chef Rupert Rowley's cooking constantly evolving. Heavily relying on British produce he fuses modern and classic dishes. Executive Chef Max, who has held a Michelin Star since 1994, tends a much admired garden that provides fruit, vegetables and herbs for the kitchen.

RISLEY HALL HOTEL AND SPA

DERBY ROAD, RISLEY, DERBYSHIRE DE72 3SS
Tel: 0115 939 9000 **International:** +44 (0)115 939 9000
Web: www.condenastjohansens.com/risleyhall **E-mail:** reservations.risleyhall@ohiml.com

Our inspector loved: *The Baronial Hall with its Minstrels' Gallery.*

Price Guide:
single from £110
double from £125
suite from £140

Awards/Recognition: 1 AA Rosette 2011–2012

Location: A52, 1 mile; M1 jct 25, 1 miles; Nottingham/Derby, 7 miles; East Midlands International Airport, 10 miles

Attractions: Donnington Park; Twycross Zoo; Chatsworth House; Nottingham Castle and Tales of Robin Hood

Risley Hall is a delightful manor house hotel dating back as far as the 11th century and is set in 10 acres of well-tended gardens. The traditional décor transports you to a bygone era with a charming combination of features from the Victorian period alongside art-nouveau influenced woodwork details, pretty wallpapers and open fireplaces. You can admire the view across the lawns and hedges from the bay window in the drawing room, or the snug bar that is perfect for pre-dinner drinks. The restaurant is set over 4 rooms which include the atmospheric Oak Room with its panelling, impressive windows and fire place. Bedrooms are very comfortable and vary in style and character with many affording wonderful garden views. If you wish to be pampered during your stay, the hotel's Elemis spa and team of therapists will indulge you with soothing treatments, or you simply enjoy a swim or soak in the Jacuzzi.

NORTHCOTE MANOR COUNTRY HOUSE HOTEL

BURRINGTON, UMBERLEIGH, DEVON EX37 9LZ
Tel: 01769 560501 **International:** +44 (0)1769 560501
Web: www.condenastjohansens.com/northcotemanor **E-mail:** rest@northcotemanor.co.uk

Our inspector loved: *The warm ambience, friendly service and contemporary yet traditional feel of this homely country house.*

Price Guide:
single from £110
double from £160
suite from £260
four poster from £160

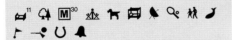

Awards/Recognition: 2 AA Rosettes 2011-2012

Location: Do not enter Burrington Village, main entrance is on the A377; Barnstaple, 14 miles; Exeter, 30 miles

Attractions: RHS Rosemoor; Dartington Crystal; Dartmoor and Exmoor; Various National Trust Properties

It is easy to understand why the luxuriously appointed 18th-century Northcote Manor has won numerous accolades over the years. Following a refurbishment including a redesign of the spacious sitting rooms, hall, restaurant and bedrooms, this very special property has retained its charmingly unpretentious ambience of timeless tranquillity. Savour seasonal gourmet meals in the elegant restaurant while admiring the view of the pretty gardens, and take afternoon tea on the terrace garden that overlooks the Japanese water garden. Sitting high above the Taw River Valley you might feel like doing nothing more than playing a game of croquet, reading a book under a large shady tree or enjoying a relaxing treatment, such as Indian head massage, manicure or pedicure, in the comfort of your own room. Alternatively, there is a golf course next door, outstanding fishing at the end of the drive, tennis and the area hosts some of the best shoots in the county.

GIDLEIGH PARK

CHAGFORD, DEVON TQ13 8HH
Tel: 01647 432367 **International:** +44 (0)1647 432367
Web: www.condenastjohansens.com/gidleighpark **E-mail:** gidleighpark@gidleigh.co.uk

Our inspector loved: The excellent fine dining and attentive service make Gidleigh Park a memorable place to stay.

Price Guide:
room £310 – £1175

Awards/Recognition: Condé Nast Johansens Most Excellent Restaurant 2011; Voted Number One in the Sunday Times Top 100 Restaurants 2011; 4 AA Rosettes 2011-2012; 2 Star Michelin 2011; Relais & Châteaux

Location: A382, 2.5 miles; A30, 4.79 miles; M5 jct 31, 20 miles; Exeter St. Davids Railway Station, 21 miles; Exeter International Airport, 28.5 miles

Attractions: Castle Drogo; Dartmouth; Exeter Cathedral; Dartmoor National Park; RHS Rosemoor

Situated in the heart of Dartmoor National Park you will appreciate the family run Gidleigh Park for its outstanding international reputation for comfort and gastronomy. A clutch of top culinary awards including 2 Michelin stars for its imaginative cuisine and the wine list, make it one of the best in Britain. Service throughout the hotel is faultless. The bedrooms – 2 of them in a converted chapel – are furnished with original antiques. The public rooms are well appointed and during the cooler months, a fire burns in the lounge's impressive fireplace. Privacy is complete, amidst 107 secluded acres in the Teign Valley. A croquet lawn and a splendid water garden can be found in the grounds. A 360 yard long, par 52 putting course designed by Peter Alliss was opened in 1995.

COMBE HOUSE

GITTISHAM, HONITON, NEAR EXETER, DEVON EX14 3AD
Tel: 01404 540400 **International:** +44 (0)1404 540400
Web: www.condenastjohansens.com/combehousegittisham **E-mail:** stay@combehousedevon.com

Our inspector loved: The restored Victorian kitchen gardens. Combe House is always full of wonderful surprises excellent service and fabulous food.

Price Guide:
single from £169
double/twin £199-£369
suite £399-£419

Awards/Recognition: Condé Nast Johansens Most Excellent Country House Hotel 2010

Location: M5 jct 29, 11 miles; A303/A30, 2 miles; Exeter Airport, 10 miles; Honiton Railway Station (for London Waterloo), 4 miles

Attractions: South West Coastal Path; Sidmouth to Lyme Regis; Cathedral City of Exeter; Honiton Antique Shops and Galleries

Ken and Ruth Hunt have enjoyed 13 years of resident ownership of the grade 1 listed Combe House resulting in this very special retreat, which continues to tirelessly pursue the desire to find new ways to delight. Voted Devon's Hotel of the Year 2010 at the Devon Tourism Awards, this hidden away country house hotel with restaurant and kitchen gardens is set in 3,500 acres and is simply magical. All of the bedrooms have been refurbished and provide a stunning combination of contemporary furnishings, fine antiques and fresh flowers. A romantic thatch cottage for 2 with secure walled garden is tucked away within the estate. The 2 Master Chefs of Great Britain love to draw on the West Country's bounteous larder nearby and Combe's own gardens. Well chosen wines and generous hospitality are always on the menu. Just a short drive to the South West Coastal paths and the wide open spaces of Dartmoor.

THE TIDES REACH HOTEL

SOUTH SANDS, SALCOMBE, DEVON TQ8 8LJ

Tel: 01548 843466 **International:** +44 (0)1548 843466
Web: www.condenastjohansens.com/tidesreach **E-mail:** enquire@tidesreach.com

Our inspector loved: *The stunning setting just moments from the sea.*

Price Guide: (including dinner)
single £78–£190
double/twin £146–£380

Awards/Recognition: Condé Nast Johansens Readers Award 2009; 1 AA Rosette 2011-2012

Location: A381, 2 miles; M5, 43 miles; Salcombe, 1.7 miles; Exeter Airport, 45 miles

Attractions: Gardens of Overbecks; Plymouth Maritime Museum; South Devon Coastal Path; Dartmoor

This south-facing charming hotel sits in a sandy cove just inside the mouth of the Salcombe Estuary. Family run for over 41 years, the Edwards family have gained a reputation for warmth, hospitality and excellent service. Chef Finn Ibsen creates menus with seasonal produce and makes the most of the morning catch from the local fishermen. Most of the immaculate bedrooms come with lovely sea views and offer plenty of flexibility for families. There's an indoor pool, sauna, spa, snooker table and for the very energetic a squash court. For sailing fans why not hire a Hobie Cat, sail into Salcombe for an ice-cream or spot of shopping and then happily retreat from the hordes to the comfort of Tides Reach.

HOTEL RIVIERA

THE ESPLANADE, SIDMOUTH, DEVON EX10 8AY
Tel: 01395 515201 **International:** +44 (0)1395 515201
Web: www.condenastjohansens.com/riviera **E-mail:** enquiries@hotelriviera.co.uk

Our inspector loved: *The excellent location on Sidmouth's Esplanade and traditional feel of this timeless seaside hotel.*

Price Guide: (including 6 course dinner)
single £132–£194
double/twin £264–£368
suite £400–£420

Awards/Recognition: 1 AA Rosette 2011-2012

Location: A3052, 2.5 miles; M5 jct 30, 13 miles; Exeter Airport, 10 miles; Honiton/Exeter St Davids Railway Stations, 8/15 miles

Attractions: Killerton House and Gardens; Exeter Cathedral; Powderham Castle; Dartmoor

This most prestigious, award-winning and welcoming seaview hotel is located in Lyme Bay. Peter Wharton's Hotel Riviera is arguably one of the most comfortable and most hospitable in the region offering fine dining, a fantastic wine cellar and excellent service. The exterior, with its fine Regency façade and bow-fronted windows complements the elegance of the interior comprising handsome public rooms and beautifully appointed bedrooms, many with sea views. Perfectly located at the centre of Sidmouth's historic Georgian esplanade, and awarded 4 Stars by both the AA and Visit Britain, the Riviera is committed to providing the very highest standards of excellence. Choose to dine in the attractive salon, with panoramic views across Lyme Bay, and indulge in the superb cuisine, prepared by English and French trained chefs. The exceptional cellar will please any wine connoisseur. Festive programme and short breaks are available.

WATERSMEET HOTEL

MORTEHOE, WOOLACOMBE, DEVON EX34 7EB
Tel: 01271 870333 **International:** +44 (0)1271 870333
Web: www.condenastjohansens.com/watersmeet **E-mail:** info@watersmeethotel.co.uk

Our inspector loved: The incredible location overlooking Woolacombe beach is second to none.

Price Guide: (including dinner)
single £98–£150
double/twin £150–£340
suite £220–£360

 SPA

Awards/Recognition: 1 AA Rosette 2011-2012

Location: B3343, 2 miles; A361, 4 miles; M5 jct 27, 50 miles; Barnstaple, 15 miles

Attractions: Arlington Court; Saunton Sands Champion Golf Course; National Trust Coastal Walks; Watermouth Castle

From its elevated position at the water's edge of Combesgate Beach, Watersmeet overlooks incomparable natural beauty from one of the finest and most dramatic locations in the South West. The breathtaking views of the ever-changing, rugged coastline over to Lundy Island can be admired from large picture windows in the reception rooms. And due to a refurbishment, many of the guest rooms now have balconies with sea views, and of course, all the accruements for luxury living. Take lunch and tea al fresco on the terrace or in the tea garden and dine by candlelight while watching the sunset at the pavilion restaurant. The award-winning cuisine is well-balanced, imaginative and features local ingredients. Recreational facilities include a heated outdoor pool, indoor pool with hot spa, a steam room, coastal walks along National Trust land, Saunton Sands Championship Golf Course and the sandy beach below reached via steps directly from the hotel.

CAPTAINS CLUB HOTEL & SPA

WICK FERRY, WICK LANE, CHRISTCHURCH, DORSET BH23 1HU

Tel: 01202 475111 **International:** +44 (0)1202 475111
Web: www.condenastjohansens.com/captainsclubhotel **E-mail:** enquiries@captainsclubhotel.com

Our inspector loved: *The comfortable beds, breakfast on the terrace and waterside views all made this a great place to stay.*

Price Guide: (room only)
single £169
double £169-£229
suite/apartment £289-£649

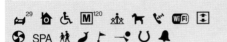

Awards/Recognition: 2 AA Rosettes 2011-2012

Location: A35, 5 min-drive; Christchurch Railway Station, 1 mile; Bournemouth, 6 miles; Bournemouth International Airport, 15 min-drive

Attractions: Christchurch Priory; Christchurch Harbour; River and Sea Cruise; New Forest National Park

Sleek, smooth and ultra modern, Captain's Club Hotel is a testament to designer flair. This strikingly contemporary luxury boutique 4 star hotel resides on the banks of the River Stour, an interesting short walk from Christchurch. Among the multitude of offerings, enjoy soothing spa treatments, trips across the bay aboard the hotel's 34-foot luxury motor cruiser, strolling along the quayside to the historic town's priory church - which boasts choir stalls older than those in Westminster Abbey - and sitting back in a so-comfortable armchair to absorb superb vistas through floor-to-ceiling windows. Each bedroom and suite has been decorated in a maritime theme, features cutting-edge amenities and looks out to a stunning riverside view. The restaurant's cuisine reflects the feel of the hotel: uncomplicated, fresh, innovative and ultimately satisfying. The afternoon tea platter is a must!

Christchurch Harbour Hotel & Spa

95 MUDEFORD, CHRISTCHURCH, DORSET BH23 3NT
Tel: 01202 483434 **International:** +44 (0)1202 483434
Web: www.condenastjohansens.com/christchurchharbour **E-mail:** christchurch@harbourhotels.co.uk

Our inspector loved: *The beautiful coastal location and taking lunch on the terrace whilst absorbing the view.*

Price Guide: (including dinner)
single £125-£185
double £145-£230

Awards/Recognition: 2 AA Rosettes 2011-2012

Location: Avon Beach, 0.5 miles; Bournemouth, 10 miles; Southampton, 25 miles; London, 80 miles

Attractions: New Forest; Isle of Wight; Hengistbury Head; Avon Beach

Close to the world famous Dorset Heritage Coast, Bournemouth and New Forest National Park, Christchurch Harbour Hotel has recently been renovated to provide luxury accommodation, with many rooms and public spaces boasting picturesque views across Mudeford Quay towards Hengistbury Head. While sophisticated, the hotel is relaxed, and with its purposefully designed spa on-site to nourish your body and soul, you will have no choice but to indulge and unwind. Bedrooms vary in shape and size and all are tastefully decorated in a contemporary style complete with facilities such as WiFi, flat-screen TVs and iPod docking stations. With the beach just a walk away, this is an ideal location for wonderful family holidays. Dining here is a treat – not only can you eat by the waterside at the Harbour Restaurant and Terrace but a wander into the grounds will lead you to the jetty, an informal relaxed restaurant headed up by Alex Aitkin.

SUMMER LODGE COUNTRY HOUSE HOTEL, RESTAURANT AND SPA

9 FORE STREET, EVERSHOT, DORSET DT2 0JR
Tel: 01935 482000 **International:** +44 (0)1935 482000
Web: www.condenastjohansens.com/summerlodge **E-mail:** summerlodge@rchmail.com

Our inspector loved: A drink in the warm and cosy bar before enjoying the excellent cuisine and service.

Price Guide:
single from £195
double/twin £225–£360
suite/master bedroom £425–£495

Awards/Recognition: Condé Nast Johansens Most Outstanding Service 2010; Relais & Châteaux; 3 AA Rosettes 2011-2012

Location: A37, 1.5 miles; M5 jct 25, 33.5 miles; Dorchester, 13 miles; Bournemouth, 46 miles

Attractions: Thomas Hardy Country; Cerne Abbas; Abbotsbury and Heritage Coast; Sherborne and Shaftesbury

Summer Lodge is the ultimate escape to the English countryside, nestled in 4 acres of breathtaking gardens in the heart of Wessex. Built in 1789 for the second Earl of Ilchester, it was then renovated by local architect and novelist Thomas Hardy, and was a private residence for over 200 years. A proud member of Relais and Châteaux, it offers a relaxing ambience, courtesy, comfort, exceptional cuisine and service, and feels more like a home than a hotel. The bedrooms, suites and cottages are tastefully decorated and combine the finest English furnishings with the latest technology, including free WiFi. The award-winning restaurant, under Head Chef Steven Titman and world renowned Sommelier Eric Zwiebel, serves delicious cuisine, using the abundant fresh local produce and the hotel's own herb garden; the traditional Dorset cream teas are legendary. There is also a magnificent glass-covered pool, health spa and gym, a tennis court, croquet lawn and bicycles.

Alexandra Hotel and Restaurant

POUND STREET, LYME REGIS, DORSET DT7 3HZ

Tel: 01297 442010 **International:** +44 (0)1297 442010

Web: www.condenastjohansens.com/hotelalexandra **E-mail:** enquiries@hotelalexandra.co.uk

Set in an elevated position close to the centre of Lyme Regis, this welcoming family run hotel enjoys a sensational seaview of Lyme Bay and the famous Cobb Harbour. Dating from the 18th century, the "Alex" was once the home of the Dowager Countess Poulett and, later Duc de Stacpoole, and has been a hotel since the 1900s. History and tradition are an integral part of its very English charm, and a recent refurbishment has injected a fresh, contemporary look to the lounge, reception areas, and the majority of the guest rooms, many of which overlook the sea beyond pretty lawned gardens. Enjoy the coastal views, among the best in the country, from a fabulous new deck area, the perfect spot for a light lunch, Dorset cream tea or pre-dinner cocktail. There are 2 restaurants, the sunny Conservatory and the more formal Alexandra. Both capitalise on the region's fresh, local produce. A perfect base for exploring the beaches and dramatic scenery of the Jurassic Coast.

Our inspector loved: The great views and deck area make this an ideal spot for a cream tea or a pre-dinner cocktail.

Price Guide:
single from £80
double £125-£215

Awards/Recognition: Condé Nast Johansens Most Excellent Waterside Hotel 2011

Location: On the A3052; A35, 3 miles; Honiton, 11 miles

Attractions: South West Coast Path; Philpot Museum; Fossil Walks; Marine Aquarium; Seaton Tramway

THE PRIORY HOTEL

CHURCH GREEN, WAREHAM, DORSET BH20 4ND
Tel: 01929 551666 **International:** +44 (0)1929 551666
Web: www.condenastjohansens.com/priorywareham **E-mail:** reservations@theprioryhotel.co.uk

Our inspector loved: The Priory is timeless and always a relaxing place to stay. Comfortable rooms, friendly service and a perfect riverside location.

Price Guide:
single from £164
double £205-£300
twin £300
suite £335-£360

Location: A352, 2-min drive; M27 jct 1, 50-min drive; Poole, 20-min drive; Bournemouth International Airport, 35-min drive

Attractions: Corfe Castle; National Trust beaches & nature reserves of Studland; World Heritage Jurassic Coast; Poole Harbour & Quayside

Since the 1500s, the one time Lady St Mary Priory has offered sanctuary to travellers. Located in the heart of Thomas Hardy's Dorset, it stands in immaculate gardens on the bank of the placid River Frome. The Priory Hotel underwent a sympathetic conversion and the result is an unpretentiously charming Dorset hotel, perfect for a romantic break or as a base for exploring the Jurassic Coast and Isle of Purbeck. The bedrooms are distinctively styled and feature family antiques; many rooms have views of the Purbeck Hills. A 16th century clay barn has been transformed into the Boathouse, creating 4 spacious luxury suites at the river's edge. The drawing room, residents' lounge and intimate bar create a convivial atmosphere. The Garden Room restaurant is open for breakfast and lunch, while splendid dinners are served in the vaulted stone cellars. There are moorings for guests arriving by boat.

ROCKLIFFE HALL HOTEL, GOLF & SPA

HURWORTH-ON-TEES, NEAR DARLINGTON, DURHAM DL2 2DU
Tel: 01325 729999 **International:** +44 (0)1325 729999
Web: www.condenastjohansens.com/rockliffehall **E-mail:** enquiries@rockliffehall.com

Our inspector loved: The challenging golf course and relaxing spa at this luxurious resort.

Price Guide:
single £180-£255
double £270-£430
suite £350-£430

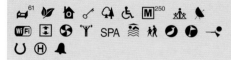

Set amidst 375 acres of beautiful North Yorkshire countryside, and with its own championship golf course on the doorstep, this 5 star luxury hotel was built as a private mansion in 1863 and is now at the centre of one of the finest resort destinations in the North of England. The Hall's history can be glimpsed in numerous period details and original features, such as carved stone pillars, oak balustrades and ornate ceilings. As befits a resort with such a contemporary, elegant and relaxed ambience, service and attention to detail are simply outstanding, as is Michelin-Starred Chef Kenny Atkinson's refined, modern British cuisine. One of the largest in the country, the hotel's stunning spa offers an impressive array of pampering treatments and activities in the state-of-the-art technogym and kinesis studio.

Awards/Recognition: Condé Nast Johansens and Corinthia Hotels Most Excellent MICE Awards, Venues that Accommodate Groups of Under 100, 2011; 3 AA Rosette 2011-2012

Location: A167, 1 mile; A1(M), 5 miles; Darlington, 5 miles; Durham Tees Valley Airport, 6 miles

Attractions: North East Coast; Newcastle-upon-Tyne; Yorkshire Dales; York and Durham

BIBURY COURT

BIBURY, GLOUCESTERSHIRE GL7 5NT
Tel: 01285 740337 **International:** +44 (0)1285 740337
Web: www.condenastjohansens.com/biburycourt **E-mail:** info@biburycourt.com

Our inspector loved: The beautifully refurbished rooms, and the new bar is a great place for a pre-dinner drink.

Price Guide:
single £150
double from £150
suite £425

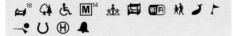

Awards/Recognition: 2 AA Rosettes 2011-2012

Location: Just off B4425; A40, 8.5 miles; Cirencester, 7 miles; Cheltenham, 22 miles

Attractions: Stow-on-the-Wold; Bourton-on-the-Water; Arlington Row; Hidcote Manor Gardens

Bibury Court is a stunning Jacobean mansion located in the beautiful Cotswold village of Bibury. Focusing on good food and fine wines, the hotel uses the best of local produce in its menus, ranging from light lunchtime dishes to haute cuisine at dinner. Whether for business or pleasure, it is the perfect location and setting for a romantic weekend, family holiday or business function. The interior is an eclectic mix of traditional grandeur mixed with new cutting edge design. All 18 bedrooms are unique, many with four poster beds, and for those who really want a treat there is the very spacious King James 1 Suite, complete with a wet room shower and marble infinity bath. The hotel's 6 acres of stunning landscaped grounds are the ideal setting for any outdoor event or wedding. Guests can take afternoon tea in the secluded areas of the garden, walk through the orchard or indulge in a spot of fishing on the River Coln.

BARNSLEY HOUSE

BARNSLEY, CIRENCESTER, GLOUCESTERSHIRE GL7 5EE
Tel: 01285 740000 **International:** +44 (0)1285 740000
Web: www.condenastjohansens.com/barnsleyhouse **E-mail:** info@barnsleyhouse.com

Our inspector loved: The small but beautiful spa adds to the tranquil atmosphere making this the perfect retreat.

Price Guide:
superior £275-£325
stableyard suite £365-£415
deluxe garden suite £495-£545

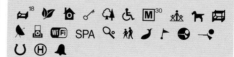

Surrounded by enchanting gardens and ancient meadows, this charming Cotswolds hotel has a style of its own. Built as a private house in the 17th century by the local squire, it is now a stylish, character-filled country home that you can comfortably retreat to for a tranquil break or invigorating spa weekend. The superb gardens and grounds attract thousands of paying visitors but they do not encroach on the privacy and required standards for you as a hotel guest. The focus at Barnsley House is on comfort, luxury, service, good food and wine in congenial surroundings. Traditional stone fireplaces, wood floors and heavy beams merge with contemporary furnishings and 21st-century facilities. Bedrooms are a testament to modern design, the cuisine is sumptuous and a big screen cinema room is available for you to sit back and view films at selected times.

Location: M4 J15, 25-min drive; Bibury, 8-min drive; Cirencester, 10-min drive; Kemble Railway Station, 15-min drive; Bristol Airport, 90-min drive

Attractions: Bibury Village; Cirencester; Cheltenham

Lower Slaughter Manor

LOWER SLAUGHTER, GLOUCESTERSHIRE GL54 2HP
Tel: 01451 820456 **International:** +44 (0)1451 820456
Web: www.condenastjohansens.com/lowerslaughtermanor **E-mail:** info@lowerslaughter.co.uk

Our inspector loved: *The beautiful, contemporary interiors mixed with the style and tradition of this perfectly restored grade 2 listed manor house.*

Price Guide:
single from £230
double £310–£420
suite £370–£880

Awards/Recognition: Relais & Châteaux; 3 AA Rosettes 2011-2012

Location: A429, 0.5 miles; Stow-on-the-Wold, 4 miles; M5 jct 10, 20 miles; Cheltenham, 21 miles

Attractions: Blenheim Palace; Stratford-upon-Avon; Warwick Castle; Sudeley Castle; The Cotswolds; Regency Cheltenham and Racecourse; Dreamy Spires of Oxford

In the heart of the incredible picturesque Cotswold village of Lower Slaughter, this beautifully restored grade 2 listed country manor house hotel positively oozes style. A contemporary feel teases the house's historic character and its "designer" bedrooms are chic and continental in flavour. Here detail is exceptional with beautiful linen, eclectic pieces of art and wall mounted iPod docking stations. Enjoy the exquisite cuisine alongside a well balanced list of specially selected wines from the Old and New Worlds. The wonderful grounds feature a croquet lawn and, within the delightful walled garden, a unique 2-storey dovecote that dates back to the 15th century. This is a wonderful setting for private parties, business meetings, weddings and civil partnership ceremonies.

WASHBOURNE COURT

LOWER SLAUGHTER, GLOUCESTERSHIRE GL54 2HS
Tel: 01451 822143 **International:** +44 (0)1451 822143
Web: www.condenastjohansens.com/washbournecourt **E-mail:** info@washbournecourt.co.uk

Our inspector loved: The attractive setting ensuring a thoroughly relaxing experience and good company.

Price Guide: (including dinner)
single from £135
double/twin £185-£325
suite £235-£385

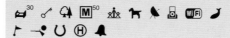

Awards/Recognition: 2 AA Rosettes 2011-2012

Location: A429, 0.5 miles; Bourton-on-the-Water, 2 miles

Attractions: Cheltenham Race Course; Batsford Arboretum; Cotswold Wildlife Park; Sudeley Castle; Stratford-upon-Avon

Washbourne Court offers a unique and refreshing twist on a luxury country house hotel. Located on the winning 2011 Google Street View Awards' Most Romantic Street in Britain, in the heart of the beautiful village of Lower Slaughter, this 17th-century riverside hotel stands in 4 acres of grounds alongside the River Eye. Its inspired mix of exciting contemporary design and historic features include traditional beamed ceilings, stone mullioned windows and a magnificent fireplace in the lounge. The fashionable Eton's Restaurant, luxuriously relaxing Scholar's Lounge and the riverside terrace, serve seasonally changing menus of modern British cuisine with an emphasis on the best local ingredients. The designer bedrooms are sophisticated yet informal incorporating flat-screen TVs, iPod docking stations and DVD players; an understated blend of the authentic and funky, creating the ultimate Cotswold retreat.

BURLEIGH COURT

BURLEIGH, MINCHINHAMPTON, NEAR STROUD, GLOUCESTERSHIRE GL5 2PF

Tel: 01453 883804 **International:** +44 (0)1453 883804

Web: www.condenastjohansens.com/burleighgloucestershire **E-mail:** burleighcourt@aol.com

Our inspector loved: The relaxed atmosphere, beautiful grounds and far reaching hill top views.

Price Guide:
single £90-£110
double £140-£160
suite £200

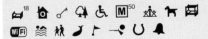

Awards/Recognition: 2 AA Rosettes 2011-2012

Location: A419, 0.5 miles; M4 jct, 28.5 miles; Cirencester, 11.5 miles; Cheltenham, 16 miles

Attractions: Cotswolds; Bath; Slimbridge Wildfowl Trust; Westonbirt Arboretum

Journey through honey-stoned Cotswold villages to reach this 18th-century former gentleman's manor that is now a charming hotel. Nestling on a steep hillside overlooking the Golden Valley its relaxed atmosphere and acres of beautifully tended gardens featuring terraces, ponds, pools, hidden pathways and Cotswold stone walls create an idyllic setting. Many bedrooms in the main house have garden views though for families we recommend the coach house rooms, located by a Victorian plunge pool as well as those within the courtyard gardens which offer flexible accommodation. The restaurant has a reputation for classical dishes and a wine cellar to satisfy the most demanding drinker. From here you can easily explore the market towns of Minchinhampton, Tetbury, Cirencester, Painswick and Bibury.

THE MANOR HOUSE HOTEL

MORETON-IN-MARSH, GLOUCESTERSHIRE GL56 0LJ

Tel: 01608 650501 **International:** +44 (0)1608 650501

Web: www.condenastjohansens.com/manorhousemoreton **E-mail:** info@manorhousehotel.info

Our inspector loved: The excellent location combined with the lovely gardens, contemporary interiors and friendly service.

Price Guide:
double/twin £155-£260
suite £290-£330

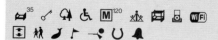

Awards/Recognition: 2 AA Rosettes 2011-2012

Location: On the A429; M40, jct 8/15, 22 miles; Cheltenham, 20 miles; Birmingham International Airport, 40 miles

Attractions: Cheltenham Races, Bath and Oxford; Stratford-upon-Avon; Blenheim Palace; Westonbirt Concerts and Events

Dating back to the 16th century, this enchanting 4 star hotel in the heart of England is steeped in a fine history that is reflected in its décor, its sensitive refurbishment and exceptional hospitality. On entering you cannot help but be impressed by the effortless combination of plush fabrics, elegant furnishings and practical contemporary convenience. The atmosphere is informal and friendly, where nothing is too much trouble. If it's a nice day take a stroll through the secluded garden filled with sweet scented flowers and meandering pathways to discover a 300-year-old mulberry tree and mature evergreen oak, or soak up the warmth on the sun terrace - the perfect place for an evening cocktail. The award-winning restaurant is a special treat where most of the produce is local with seasonal twists that remind you of your countryside location. The hotel is also ideal for small board meetings for up to 10 and can host up to 120 for presentations and conferences.

CALCOT MANOR HOTEL & SPA

NEAR TETBURY, GLOUCESTERSHIRE GL8 8YJ
Tel: 01666 890391 **International:** +44 (0)1666 890391
Web: www.condenastjohansens.com/calcotmanor **E-mail:** reception@calcotmanor.co.uk

Our inspector loved: *The superb spa and family-friendly facilities. There is something for everyone here - an always relaxing and very special place to stay.*

Price Guide:
double/twin £240-£295
family room from £295
family suite from £340

Awards/Recognition: Condé Nast Johansens Most Excellent Family Hotel 2010; 2 AA Rosettes 2011-2012

Location: On the A4135; Tetbury, 3.5 miles; M5 jct 13, 11 miles; M4 jct 18, 12.5 miles

Attractions: Westonbirt Arboretum; Bath; Cotswolds; Cirencester

Calcot Manor is an enchanting Cotswolds hotel set in over 200 acres of meadowland. Dating back to the 14th-century, it boasts 700 years of history; the original building was erected in 1300AD! Further to a sensitive refurbishment, it is now a luxurious haven offering extensive facilities and spacious, individually and tastefully designed bedrooms with every modern comfort. Calcot also has a crèche and wonderful facilities for families, including dedicated family rooms and suites. Enjoy gourmet dishes at the Conservatory Restaurant whilst gazing over delightful countryside views. However, if you're in the mood for traditional pub meals, then the exceptional Gumstool Inn is for you; its wonderful sun terrace is the perfect spot for al fresco dining. Be sure to visit the spa, a welcome retreat providing a wide range of therapies as well as a gymnasium, hot tub and pool.

LIME WOOD

BEAULIEU ROAD, LYNDHURST, HAMPSHIRE SO43 7FZ
Tel: 023 8028 7177 **International:** +44 (0)23 8028 7177
Web: www.condenastjohansens.com/limewood **E-mail:** info@limewood.co.uk

Our inspector loved: Everything about this modern classic, from the beautiful spa to the sumptuous rooms.

Price Guide:
eaves £245-£295
generous £395-£445
forest suites £445-£775

Set in the heart of the New Forest, and within easy driving distance from London, this child-friendly 5 star luxury hotel is the perfect destination for a weekend getaway or a family break. Built as a hunting lodge in the 13th century, this luxurious Regency-style country house hotel was recently renovated with a fresh approach, reviving its original architecture and grounds, yet keeping its charm and character. The generously sized bedrooms and suites are filled with indulgent touches, antiques and hand-picked pieces of art; some have a log fire or wood burning stove. Activities include yoga and bike riding, and for relaxation, there is a state-of-the-art spa with swimming pool, hydrotherapy pool and saunas. Head Chef Luke Holder creates imaginative hearty British fare based on local organic produce, served in the glamorous Dining Room or the more informal setting of The Scullery.

Awards/Recognition: Condé Nast Johansens Taittinger Wine List Awards, Special Commendation Connoisseurs List 2011; Relais & Châteaux; 3 AA Rosettes 2011-2012

Location: A31, 0.5 miles; Lyndhurst, 1.5 miles; London, 1.30-min drive; Southampton, 12 miles

Attractions: New Forest National Park; Highcliffe Beach; Motor Museum, Beaulieu; Lymington; Foraging

CHEWTON GLEN

NEW MILTON, NEW FOREST, HAMPSHIRE BH25 6QS
Tel: 01425 275341 **International:** +44 (0)1425 275341 **US Toll Free:** 1 800 344 5087
Web: www.condenastjohansens.com/chewtonglen **E-mail:** reservations@chewtonglen.com

Our inspector loved: Vetiver, the new restaurant offering a choice of dining options.

Price Guide:
bronze from £250
suites from £486

Awards/Recognition: Condé Nast Johansens Most Excellent Hotel 2010; Relais & Châteaux; 3 AA Rosettes 2011-2012;

Location: Heathrow, 85 miles; M27 jct 1, 14 miles; Southampton Airport, 26 miles; Mainline Train Station, 2 miles

Attractions: New Forest National Park; Isle of Wight; Bournemouth; Lymington

Arrive with exceptional expectations and you certainly won't be disappointed. Chewton Glen is set in 130 acres of gardens and parkland on the edge of the New Forest, not far from the sea. Bedrooms are the ultimate in luxury, with marble bathrooms, cosy bathrobes and views over the grounds. Try Vetiver, the new dining experience where Executive Chef Luke Matthews creates surprising and innovative dishes from fresh local produce alongside an impressive wine list. And allow yourself to be seduced by the stunning spa, with its magnificent 17-metre swimming pool, steam, sauna, treatment rooms, gym and hydrotherapy pool. Outside there's another pool, sun terrace, croquet lawn, tennis and a 9-hole par 3 course. What more could you really want?

TYLNEY HALL

ROTHERWICK, HOOK, HAMPSHIRE RG27 9AZ
Tel: 01256 764881 **International:** +44 (0)1256 764881
Web: www.condenastjohansens.com/tylneyhall **E-mail:** reservations@tylneyhall.com

Our inspector loved: The beautiful terrace overlooking the extensive gardens and parkland.

Price Guide:
double/twin £220–£360
suite £430–£500

Awards/Recognition: 2 AA Rosettes 2011-2012

Location: A30, 1 mile; M3 jct5, 3 miles; Basingstoke, 6.5 miles; Heathrow, 32 miles

Attractions: Watercress Line steam railway; Historic Cathedral City of Winchester; West Green House and Gardens; Jane Austen's House

Arriving at Tylney Hall in the evening, with its floodlit forecourt fountain, it is easy to imagine attending a private party in a stately home. Set in 66 acres of ornamental gardens and parkland, this impressive Grade II listed mansion typifies the great houses of another era. The bedrooms are luxuriously appointed; some have four-poster beds and spa baths. Food plays a big part here; guests can enjoy exquisite meals in the award-winning Oak Room Restaurant or on the terrace during summer. Surrounding the hotel are beautiful wooded trails ideal for jogging, a lake with boathouse bridge, an orchard and Victorian greenhouses. The leisure facilities include 2 swimming pools, all-weather tennis courts, croquet, snooker and mountain bike hire, whilst golf is available at the adjacent 18-hole golf course. The health spa offers four treatment rooms, gym, saunas and whirlpool. Weddings, conferences and special events can be held in the 12 private banqueting rooms.

CASTLE HOUSE

CASTLE STREET, HEREFORD, HEREFORDSHIRE HR1 2NW
Tel: 01432 356321 **International:** +44 (0)1432 356321
Web: www.condenastjohansens.com/castlehse **E-mail:** info@castlehse.co.uk

Our inspector loved: The delicious dinner of locally sourced produce and ingredients, much from the owner's own farm.

Price Guide:
single £130
double £190
suite £195–£230

Awards/Recognition: 2 AA Rosettes 2011-2012

Location: Off the A438; A49, 0.8 miles; M4 jct 20, 43 miles

Attractions: Mappa Mundi and Chained Library at Hereford Cathedral; Ludlow; Hay on Wye; Cheltenham

This townhouse hotel, with Rosette-awarded restaurant, is a testament to luxury boutique style located in the heart of the city, just 100m from Hereford Cathedral. Step though the door of the immaculate Georgian façade to a warm welcome and bright lobby area dominated by a grand staircase before being led to your comfortable bedroom where personal touches of fresh flowers, bowls of fruit and a filled decanter await. The Restaurant, overseen by Head Chef Claire Nicholls, serves English dishes with an international twist prepared from locally sourced produce and home-grown vegetables. In fact, most of the menu's beef and lamb have been reared on the owner's nearby farm. Especially good is the fillet of beef with sweet potato dauphinoise, caramelised shallots and wild mushroom compote. The Castle Bar and Bistro is ideal for a lighter lunch or snacks. A beautifully landscaped garden runs down to the old castle moat and is perfect for enjoying afternoon tea.

THE GEORGE OF STAMFORD

ST MARTINS, STAMFORD, LINCOLNSHIRE PE9 2LB
Tel: 01780 750750 **International:** +44 (0)1780 750750
Web: www.condenastjohansens.com/georgeofstamford **E-mail:** reservations@georgehotelofstamford.com

Our inspector loved: Dining al fresco in the court yard, an award winning wine list and the enthusiastic and attentive staff.

Price Guide:
single from £95
double from £150
superior from £230

As you drive along one of the most famous highways in the world, you are sure to see the "Gallows" sign for this traditional English coaching inn, a delightful hotel with over 900 years of fascinating history. A popular meeting point for the locals of Stamford and an idyllic weekend getaway destination, this is one of England's great architectural gems and purveyor of great food. The cuisine is superb, the wines are first class, and the surroundings are charming and time-honoured; a wonderful silver carving trolley is used and reminiscent of bygone days. During the warmer months, you can enjoy a meal in the courtyard. Bedrooms are very individual, some with beams or oak panelling and others in bold designer fabrics. The devotion to good hospitality is evident in every member of the team who work at this friendly, bustling hotel.

Awards/Recognition: Condé Nast Johansens Taittinger Wine List Award, Overall Winner 2010; Condé Nast Johansens Taittinger Wine List Award, Special Commendation Staff Training 2010; 1 AA Rosette 2011–2012

Location: A1, 1 mile; Peterborough, 10 miles; London, 1-hour train ride

Attractions: The Architectural Gem of Stamford; Burghley House; Rutland Water; Market Towns of Oakham & Uppingham

LONDON - BUCKINGHAM PALACE

41

41 BUCKINGHAM PALACE ROAD, LONDON SW1W 0PS
Tel: 020 7300 0041 **International:** +44 (0)20 7300 0041
Web: www.condenastjohansens.com/41buckinghampalaceroad **E-mail:** book41@rchmail.com

Our inspector loved: *This absolute gem and our top London award winner!*

Price Guide:
king-size bedroom from £295
junior suite £499
master suite £699

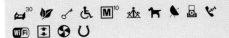

Awards/Recognition: Condé Nast Johansens Most Excellent London Hotel 2011

Location: Victoria Station, 5-min walk; St Pancras/Eurostar, 3.6 miles; Heathrow Airport, 15 miles; Gatwick Airport, 23 miles; Stansted Airport, 37 miles

Attractions: Buckingham Palace; London Eye; Houses of Parliament; Hyde Park

This boutique hotel of splendid luxury overlooks the Royal Mews and was voted TripAdvisor's No 1 London Hotel 2009. Within a 2-minute walk of Buckingham Palace and Victoria Station, this exclusive little gem is renowned for its exceptional value, caring service, generous hospitality and thoughtful touches. Beyond the striking architecture is a black and white themed interior design where distinguishing features and services such as a choice of turndown options, an honesty bar and 24-hour informal dining, make guests feel truly at home; there is even a pantry filled with tasty home-made treats for a midnight feast! Bedrooms and suites are furnished in hand carved mahogany and black leather, feature iPod docking stations, movies, music, free WiFi and extravagantly comfortable hand stitched English mattresses. Next door is the cosy Leopard Bar, the more traditional Library Restaurant and bbar for exotic cocktails and South African fusion cuisine.

CHEVAL PHOENIX HOUSE

1 WILBRAHAM PLACE, SLOANE STREET, LONDON, SW1X 9AE
Tel: 020 7259 8222 **International:** +44 (0)20 7259 8222
Web: www.condenastjohansens.com/phoenixhouse **E-mail:** cph@chevalresidences.com

Our inspector loved: The duplex with sophisticated minimalism.

Price Guide: (per night, excluding VAT, minimum 7-night stay. Full T&C's available)
studio from £185
1 bedroom apt from £250
1 bedroom duplex from £340
2 bedroom apt from £364
2 x 1 interconnect duplex from £750

Location: Sloane Square Tube Station, 5-min walk

Attractions: Royal Court Theatre; Sloane Square; Saatchi Gallery; Le Cercle Restaurant

The award-winning, charming Cheval Phoenix House is nestled in the heart of Chelsea. A private residence with attentive 24-hour concierge service, it is an exclusive gateway to one of London's most desirable neighbourhoods, just minutes from the boutiques and galleries of Sloane Square, close to Duke of York Square and designer shops at Chelsea Harbour. After a long day of Chelsea living indulge in opulent organic hampers, pamper yourself with Aveda toiletries and rest in sumptuous beds fitted with fine Frette linens. Each residence is a stylish setting for entertaining but if you'd rather dine out, the innovative Le Cercle restaurant is on the doorstep. Try the superb French grazing menu or enlist the skill of a Le Cercle chef in the privacy of your residence. Available as studios, 1 or 2-bedroom apartments and duplexes, Cheval Phoenix House offers a variety of accommodation to suit a range of requirements, for short breaks or longer stays.

The Wyndham Grand London Chelsea Harbour

CHELSEA HARBOUR, LONDON SW10 0XG
Tel: 020 7823 3000 **International:** +44 (0)20 7823 3000
Web: www.condenastjohansens.com/wyndhamlondon **E-mail:** wyndhamlondon@wyndham.com

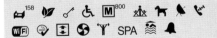

Our inspector loved: *The location and wonderful facilities.*

Price Guide:
suite £192
penthouse from £1,500

Awards/Recognition: 1 AA Rosette 2011–2012

Location: Imperial Wharf Railway Station, 5-min walk; London St Pancras, 7 miles; London Heathrow Airport, 14 miles

Attractions: Chelsea Harbour Design Centre; Harrods; Harvey Nichols; King's Road; Westfield Shopping Centre

A unique hotel for London, The Wyndham Grand is an impressive five star, all suite property that sits proudly overlooking the boats moored in exclusive Chelsea Harbour. Its West London location is ideal for a break exploring all the central London sites and shopping on the King's Road and Sloane Street. The suites are spacious, immaculate and the detail reflects thoughtful consideration for the seasoned traveller, or you can enjoy elevated luxury in the Penthouses with panoramic views and unique art. There is something incredibly relaxing about dining at the award-winning restauraunt Chelsea Riverside Brasserie, where you can dine outside on warm days. You get a feeling that you are anywhere other than a city centre, yet a short ride in the river launch will take city travellers right to the centre of the Docklands, whilst the more fashion conscious will enjoy the chauffeur service to the heart of Knightsbridge.

CHEVAL CALICO HOUSE

42 BOW LANE, LONDON EC4M 9DT
Tel: 020 7489 2500 **International:** +44 (0)20 7489 2500
Web: www.condenastjohansens.com/calicohouse **E-mail:** cch@chevalresidences.com

Our inspector loved: Rubbing shoulders with historic London.

Price Guide: (per night, excluding VAT, minimum 7-night stay. Full T&C's available)
studio from £125
1 bedroom apt from £142
2 bedroom apt from £184
2 bedroom executive apt from £248
2 bedroom penthouse from £233

The City is the beating heart of London, home to St Paul's Cathedral, the Tate Modern, Bank of England and the Barbican arts complex. Located just off Bow Lane is the exclusive Cheval Calico House comprising elegant studios and 1 and 2-bedroom apartments. Equally ideal as a base for business and pleasure, the apartments are available for both short and extended stays. Guests enjoy the freedom of a private residence whilst benefiting from the convenience and facilities of a hotel. High-speed broadband access, fully-equipped kitchens, up-to-date audio-visual equipment, 24-hour concierge, on-site management and a daily maid service ensure that your stay is a memorable and enjoyable one.

Location: Mansion House Tube Station, 5-min walk; London City Airport, 7 miles; Heathrow Airport, 18 miles; Eurostar St Pancras, 2 miles

Attractions: St Pauls Cathedral; Tower of London; Borough Market; Shopping

THE MAYFLOWER HOTEL

26-28 TREBOVIR ROAD, LONDON SW5 9NJ
Tel: 020 7370 0991 **International:** +44 (0)20 7370 0991
Web: www.condenastjohansens.com/mayflower **E-mail:** info@mayflower-group.co.uk

Our inspector loved: *Comfort, style and good value for money.*

Price Guide:
double £120-£155
suite £130-£195

Awards/Recognition: 4 AA Rosettes 2011-2012

Location: Earls Court Underground Station, 2-min walk; M4 jct1, 8 miles; Heathrow Airport, 14 miles; Waterloo International, 5 miles

Attractions: Buckingham Palace; Harrods; Victoria and Albert Museum; Hyde Park

Great value for money, The Mayflower townhouse hotel is a wonderful example of Eastern influences in the centre of London. Full of originality, this is the perfect haven if you're travelling alone or on business, the guest rooms on the ground floor are small yet stylish and rich in pale stone, vibrant fabrics and Indian and Oriental antiques. Johansens guests preferring more space however, should ask for one of the first floor bedrooms - refurbished in light, fresh colours with sparkling glass lighting and mirrors. Stylish bathrooms sparkle with slate and chrome and have walk in showers. A continental buffet breakfast is served in the downstairs dining room, or when the weather is fine, in the new extended patio garden. You can grab a caffeine or vitamin C fix in the coffee and juice bar before heading out to Knightsbridge, Chelsea and surrounding attractions such as the Natural History and Science Museums. The hotel is close to the Earls Court Exhibition Centre.

TWENTY NEVERN SQUARE

20 NEVERN SQUARE, LONDON SW5 9PD
Tel: 020 7565 9555 **International:** +44 (0)20 7565 9555
Web: www.condenastjohansens.com/twentynevernsquare **E-mail:** hotel@twentynevernsquare.co.uk

Our inspector loved: This oasis of comfort and style close to Earls Court.

Price Guide:
double/twin £130–£165
suite £275

Location: Earls Court Underground, 2-min walk; M4, 8 miles; Heathrow Airport, 14 miles; Gatwick Airport, 35 miles

Attractions: Victoria and Albert Museum; Natural History Museum; Harrods; Hyde Park

This wonderful townhouse hotel is located close to Earls Court and Olympia Exhibition Centres, and is just 10 minutes from designer shops, restaurants, theatres and attractions such as the Victoria & Albert Musuem and the Science Museum. An elegant 4-star townhouse hotel, Twenty Nevern Square provides a unique hospitality experience. Its sumptuously restored, compact bedrooms emphasise natural materials, hand-carved beds and white marble. Choose from the delicate silks of the Chinese Room or touch of opulence in the Rococo Room. If you're looking to really spoil someone, then the grandeur and style of the new Ottoman Suite is the perfect treat! Breakfast is served in the light, bright Conservatory opening onto a decked balcony area, and gym facilities are available by arrangement.

CHEVAL GLOUCESTER PARK

ASHBURN PLACE, KENSINGTON, LONDON SW7 4LL
Tel: 020 7373 1444 **International:** +44 (0)20 7373 1444
Web: www.condenastjohansens.com/gloucesterpark **E-mail:** cgp@chevalresidences.com

Our inspector loved: The Champagne welcome hamper for longer stays.

Price Guide: (per night, excluding VAT, minimum 28-night stay. Full T&C's available)
1 bedroom apt from £225
2 bedroom apt from £283
3 bedroom apt from £492

Location: Gloucester Road Tube Station, 1-min walk; High Street Kensington Tube Station, 10-min walk

Attractions: Royal Albert Hall; Kensington Gardens; National History Museum; Shopping; Restaurants

Perfectly located in the heart of London, the unique Cheval Gloucester Park is just a short stroll from Kensington Gardens and Knightsbridge, convenient for exploring the boutiques of Kensington, Harvey Nichols, Harrod's and Hyde Park. Comfortable and spacious, each 1, 2 and 3-bedroom apartment is available for extended stays of 28 days or longer. They are intelligently designed, impeccably furnished and feature a sense of playful fun; most boast unparalleled views across London. A knowledgeable 24-hour concierge is at your disposal to help with any arrangements or reservations and a daily housekeeping service from Mondays through to Fridays maintains impeccable standards. Designed for luxury living, treat Cheval Goucester Park as your very own London home.

Cheval Thorney Court

PALACE GATE, KENSINGTON, LONDON W8 5NJ
Tel: 020 7581 5324 **International:** +44 (0)20 7581 5324
Web: www.condenastjohansens.com/thorneycourt **E-mail:** ctc@chevalresidences.com

Our inspector loved: *The wonderfully surprising spacious "country house" feel.*

Price Guide: (per night, excluding VAT, minimum 22-night stay. Full T&C's available)
2 bedroom apt £322-£572
2 bedroom penthouse from £643
3 bedroom apt £568-£779

Location: High Street Kensington Tube Station, 10-min walk; Gloucester Road Tube Station, 10-min walk

Attractions: Royal Albert Hall; Kensington Gardens; Shopping; Museums

Cheval Thorney Court effortlessly combines tradition, privacy and security. Just minutes from parks and gardens, palaces and museums, this is one of Kensington's most desirable addresses. Most of the penthouses and apartments overlook Kensington Gardens and each is furnished with a distinctly timeless Georgian elegance, Regency stripes, leather-topped writing bureaus, marble bathrooms, sumptuous dining rooms and an overall stately home ambience. Cheval Thorney Court is the perfect destination for those seeking upscale accommodation for an extended stay and a sumptuous setting for entertaining in style. The concierge desk is attended 24-hours a day and a daily maid service is in operation Mondays-Fridays.

KENSINGTON HOUSE HOTEL

15-16 PRINCE OF WALES TERRACE, KENSINGTON, LONDON W8 5PQ
Tel: 020 7937 2345 **International:** +44 (0)20 7937 2345
Web: www.condenastjohansens.com/kensingtonhouse **E-mail:** reservations@kenhouse.com

Our inspector loved: The location, just tucked away off Kensington High Street, a warm welcome and good value.

Price Guide: (including continental breakfast)
single £165
double/twin £194
executive double/twin £217
junior suites £252

Location: High Street Kensington Underground, 0.3 miles; M4, 8 miles; Heathrow, 14 miles; Gatwick, 37 miles

Attractions: Royal Albert Hall; Science Museum; Victoria and Albert Museum; Natural History Museum

Kensington House is a townhouse hotel located just off Kensington High Street overlooking delightful mews houses, leafy streets and City rooftops. The atmosphere is relaxed, the excellent service is informal yet professional, and the bright, airy bedrooms feature tall windows and modern furnishings that add freshness to practical design. You can slip between crisp linen sheets and snuggle up in cosy bathrobes, and for those travelling en famille, 2 junior suites convert into a family room. The Tiger Bar is a bright and buzzy venue to enjoy continental breakfast, coffee and drinks throughout the day, and the takeaway room service menu is popular with guests. The serenity of Kensington Gardens is just a short stroll away, while some of the capital's most fashionable shops, restaurants and cultural attractions are within walking distance.

MILESTONE HOTEL

1 KENSINGTON COURT, LONDON W8 5DL
Tel: 020 7917 1000 **International:** +44 (0)20 7917 1000 **US toll free:** 1 877 955 1515
Web: www.condenastjohansens.com/milestone **E-mail:** bookms@rchmail.com

Our inspector loved: The style of this award-winning hotel with imaginatively decorated suites. Ask for the "Mistinguette Suite" with it's own private terrace for pure romantics!

Price Guide: (room only, excluding VAT)
double £320-£495
suite £599-£899

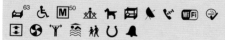

Awards/Recognition: Voted No 1 Hotel in London "Best places to Stay" Condé Nast Traveler Gold List 2011; 2 AA Rosettes 2011-2012

Location: Kensington High Street, 5-min walk; Paddington Heathrow Express, 2.18 miles; Heathrow Airport, 13.6 miles; Gatwick Airport, 37 miles

Attractions: Kensington Palace and Gardens; The Royal Albert Hall; Buckingham Palace; Harrods; The Natural History Museum

The 5 star luxury Milestone Hotel, overlooking Kensington Gardens, is in the heart of London's most exclusive shopping districts, a short walk from popular museums and only a few minutes' taxi ride from the West End. An architectural and historical treasure, its blend of personal service, splendidly luxurious accommodation and inspired cuisine has won many awards including No. 1 London Hotel on the Condé Nast Traveller Gold List 2011. Each guest room is different, dressed with fine fabrics, fresh flowers, antique furnishings and rare works of art. The club-like panelled bar is cosy and the chic black and white conservatory is ideal for intimate meetings, teas or light snacks. Sophisticated Cheneston's Restaurant serves some of the finest cuisine in the city. And the fitness centre, with resistance pool, sauna and therapy treatments, allows you to stay in shape and get pampered. The Milestone is famous for its philosophy of "no request too large, no detail too small."

BEAUFORT HOUSE

45 BEAUFORT GARDENS, KNIGHTSBRIDGE, LONDON SW3 1PN
Tel: 020 7584 2600 **International:** +44 (0)20 7584 2600
Web: www.condenastjohansens.com/beauforthouseapartments **E-mail:** info@beauforthouse.co.uk

Our inspector loved: The dedicated, attentive staff who ensure that every home comfort is available.

Price Guide: (excluding VAT)
£245–£900

Location: Knightsbridge Underground, 3-min walk; Victoria Station, 2 miles; Heathrow, 14 miles; Gatwick, 28 miles

Attractions: Harrods; Hyde Park; Buckingham Palace; Victoria and Albert Museum

Beaufort House resides on a tranquil and exclusive tree-lined Regency cul-de-sac offering 21 self-contained luxury serviced apartments, ranging from an intimate 1-bedroom to a spacious 4-bedroom apartment. Light, fresh, modish interiors are decorated in neutral tones complemented by stylish accents of colour. Kitchens are bright, crisp white spaces; very conducive to culinary creativity! Ideal for families, guests enjoy each apartment's seclusion and comfortable atmosphere of a private home with the benefits of a first-class hotel. All apartments have direct dial telephones with voice mail, safes, iPod connectors and wireless internet; some benefit from balconies or patios. The apartments are serviced daily at no additional charge and full laundry/dry cleaning services are available. The 24-hour Guests Services team is happy to organise theatre tickets, restaurant bookings and a chauffeur. Beaufort House was awarded Enjoy England's Gold Award 2011.

CHEVAL KNIGHTSBRIDGE

13 CHEVAL PLACE, LONDON, SW7 1EW
Tel: 020 7225 3325 **International:** +44 (0)20 7225 3325
Web: www.condenastjohansens.com/chevalknightsbridge **E-mail:** ck@chevalresidences.com

Our inspector loved: *The choice of locations.*

Price Guide: (per night, excluding VAT, minimum 7-night stay. Full T&C's available)
2 bedroom apt from £358
2 bedroom mews/townhouse from £372
3 bedroom apt from £500
3 bedroom townhouse/cottage from £458

Location: Knightsbridge Tube Station, 7-min walk

Attractions: Harrod's; Victoria & Albert Museum; Shopping; Restaurants

Peacefully located in an exclusive and desirable Knightsbridge neighbourhood, close to the Victoria & Albert Museum, Harvey Nichols, Hyde Park and Harrod's, is Cheval Knightsbridge Residences. Comprising mews houses, apartments, townhouses and a city cottage, guests experience the best of both worlds: the comforts of a private home coupled with the service expected from the finest hotel. Consider your chosen residence your London home; each designed with an individual style and character that can be perfectly matched to your tastes and requirements. Created for extended stays, every residence includes all your essential creature comforts such as a beautiful kitchen and the latest communication technology. A dedicated team of attentive staff is on-hand to look after every detail of your stay, leaving you free to explore your surroundings and fully immerse yourself into London life.

The Egerton House Hotel

17-19 EGERTON TERRACE, KNIGHTSBRIDGE, LONDON SW3 2BX
Tel: 020 7589 2412 **International:** +44 (0)20 7589 2412
Web: www.condenastjohansens.com/egertonhouse **E-mail:** bookeg@rchmail.com

Our inspector loved: *The fact that smart guests travel across oceans to stay here, and of course, try 1 or 2 of Antonio's magical martinis.*

Price Guide:
double/queen £280–£340
deluxe/suite £350–£610
Victoria & Albert suite £895

Awards/Recognition: Condé Nast Johansens Most Excellent London Hotel 2009

Location: Knightsbridge Underground, 5-min walk; Victoria Station, 2 miles; Heathrow, 14 miles; Gatwick, 28 miles

Attractions: Harrods; Victoria and Albert Museum; Hyde Park; Buckingham Palace

The exclusive Egerton House is perfectly situated on a secluded residential street in Knightsbridge, just a 3-minute walk from Harrods, close to the V & A Museum, Sloane Street and Central London's attractions. This enchanting Victorian house offers the ultimate "feel at home" experience with caring staff, thoughtful signature touches and splendid luxury. Each room and suite has its own character and design ranging from lavish traditional to strikingly contemporary and is adorned with exquisite furnishings, antiques and artworks that include Picasso, Braque and Matisse all complemented by modern amenities such as flat-screen TVs, free WiFi and specially programmed video iPods. Delicious breakfasts, high teas and daily specials are prepared from the finest, freshest produce and served in the charmingly sophisticated restaurant, or in the cosy, elegant lounge and bar. For martini lovers, Head Barman, Antonio Pizzuto is renowned for serving London's finest.

The Mandeville Hotel

MANDEVILLE PLACE, LONDON W1U 2BE

Tel: 020 7935 5599 **International:** +44 (0)20 7935 5599

Web: www.condenastjohansens.com/mandeville **E-mail:** sales@mandeville.co.uk

Our inspector loved: *A sense of being in exactly the right place. Plus the Men's Afternoon Teas and Robert Gaggl's innovative cocktails!*

Price Guide: (room only, excluding VAT)
single from £319
superior from £339
deluxe from £359

Awards/Recognition: 2 AA Rosette 2011–2012

Location: Bond Street Underground, 0.2 miles; Heathrow Airport, 15 miles; Victoria Station, 2 miles

Attractions: The Wallace Collection; Selfridges; Wigmore Hall; Regent's Park; Hyde Park

The Mandeville Hotel is an exciting Central London hotel with a generous helping of opulence and luxury. A very personalised service is in practise here where nothing is too much trouble for the staff. Style and sophistication is paramount throughout the hotel from the delicious terrace suite with its indulgent bathroom to decadent features and lighting in the lobby. And bedrooms are exquisitely furnished with fabrics of striking textures and tones from some of the leading London design houses. The deVille Bar at The Mandeville Hotel, is a beautifully sophisticated cocktail bar, great for meeting friends in the heart of London and now serving new organic cocktails as well as an extensive martini and mojito list. Book the Red Room for your meeting or private party, it is the perfect location, minutes from Oxford Street, Bond Street and Mayfair.

THE MAY FAIR

STRATTON STREET, MAYFAIR, LONDON W1J 8LT
Tel: 020 7769 4041 **International:** +44 (0)20 7769 4041
Web: www.condenastjohansens.com/mayfair **E-mail:** sales@themayfairhotel.co.uk

Our inspector loved: *The Schiaparelli Suite filled with Buddhist attributes, and Silvena Rowe's distinctive cuisine at Quìnce restaurant.*

Price Guide: (excluding VAT and breakfast)
king superior from £195
king deluxe from £225
studio suite from £325

Location: Green Park underground, 1-min walk; St Pancras - Eurostar, 5 miles; Heathrow, 16 miles; Gatwick, 28 miles

Attractions: Green Park; Bond Street; Royal Academy; Buckingham Palace

Stylish, contemporary and quirky, The May Fair takes 5-star luxury to another level. A legendary hotel with a glamorous past, it was first opened by King George V in 1927 and has played host to some of London's most extravagant society events. Bringing together smart and expressive modern design, outstanding service and exceptional attention to detail, the hotel fully deserves the CoolBrands 2011/12 award for the second year running, in recognition of its style and personality. A menu of over 40 expertly crafted signature drinks awaits in the renowned May Fair Bar, whilst Quìnce restaurant presents an innovative Eastern Mediterranean menu. The day spa, with its vast array of treatments, is the perfect antidote to a busy day of meetings or sightseeing, and where better to round off an eventful day than in the hotel's Palm Beach Casino, located in the former Grand Art Deco Ballroom, which offers entertainment until 6am.

WESTBURY HOTEL

BOND STREET, MAYFAIR, LONDON W1S 2YF
Tel: 020 7629 7755 **International:** +44 (0)20 7629 7755
Web: www.condenastjohansens.com/westburymayfair **E-mail:** enquiries@westburymayfair.com

Our inspector loved: *Location, service and the new Alyn Williams Michelin star restaurant.*

Price Guide: (room only)
single £399
double £439
suite from £1099

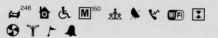

The 5 star luxury Westbury sits proudly in an enviable location just off Bond Street in the heart of London's fashionable Mayfair. The excellent personal service reflects the staff's passion to ensure every guest has a memorable stay. Complete with expert concierge and extremely adept and multi-lingual staff, this is the ideal choice for discerning guests from around the world. Bedrooms are luxuriously designed in warm tones and offer the utmost in comfort and style. Try the Gallery Restaurant with dishes inspired by the South of France and Northern Italy. A great way to start the evening is in the sophisticated Polo Bar with its impressive cocktail list and bar menu. You can see why this is popular with guests and Londoners alike.

Location: Bond Street Underground, 5-min walk; St Pancras - Eurostar, 4 miles; Heathrow Airport, 18 miles; Gatwick Airport, 30 miles

Attractions: Perfect shopping in the heart of Mayfair; West End Theatre's; National Gallery; London Eye

THE NEW LINDEN HOTEL

58 - 60 LEINSTER SQUARE, NOTTING HILL, LONDON W2 4PS
Tel: 020 7221 4321 **International:** +44 (0)20 7221 4321
Web: www.condenastjohansens.com/newlindenhotel **E-mail:** newlindenhotel@mayflower-group.co.uk

Our inspector loved: *This chic retreat in the heart of Notting Hill.*

Price Guide:
double £120-£155
suite £130-£195

Location: Notting Hill / Bayswater Tube, 5-min walk; Paddington Station, 1 mile; London Heathrow, 15 miles

Attractions: Madame Tussauds; Whiteleys of Bayswater; Hyde Park; Kensington Palace Gardens

The New Linden Hotel is a little gem with instant appeal. This pretty, white townhouse hotel is discovered in a peaceful residential street, in the heart of London's cosmopolitan Notting Hill, just a short walk from Portobello Road Market and within easy reach of tourist hot spots. The hotel's owners have transformed the building to suit the times without losing any of its Victorian charm. Once past the ornate entrance pillars you will find stylish bedrooms in colours of cream, brown, red and black, trendy minimal furnishings, high-tech entertainment units and stunning marble bathrooms. Not large, but with everything you could wish for. The lower ground floor breakfast room with its trendy wallpaper and freshly-prepared breakfast is a great place to start your day.

SOFITEL LONDON ST JAMES

6 WATERLOO PLACE, LONDON SW1Y 4AN
Tel: 020 7747 2200 **International:** +44 (0)20 7747 2200
Web: www.condenastjohansens.com/stjames **E-mail:** H3144@sofitel.com

Our inspector loved: The fact that there is always something new to indulge in, whether it's the stunning spa, stylish bedrooms, buzzing bar or a new dining experience!

Price Guide: (room only, excluding VAT)
single from £375
double from £425
suite £664-£1,800

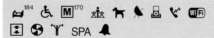

Stylish, contemporary and very imposing, Sofitel London St James in central London is a Grade II listed building on the corner of Waterloo Place and Pall Mall. This five star hotel is the former home of the Cox's & King's bank, whose original artwork is still prominently displayed. The well appointed bedrooms and suites have the smartest technology, including HD televisions. Black and white marble complements granite tops and chrome fittings in the bathrooms. French-British cuisine is trademark of the newly opened brasserie, The Balcon; while the renovated St James Bar offers a large selection of Champagnes and vintage cocktails. As for afternoon tea, you'll adore the eclectic Rose Lounge. You can also choose to relax in the stunningly designed So SPA by Sofitel or perform a full work out in the So FIT gym.

Awards/Recognition: Condé Nast Traveller Readers' Spa Awards 2011- Best UK Hotel Spa & Top 25; Condé Nast Johansens Most Excellent Spa 2010

Location: Piccadilly Underground, 3-min walk; St Pancras - Eurostar, 3 miles; Heathrow, 16 miles; Gatwick, 28 miles

Attractions: Trafalgar Square; Buckingham Palace; London Eye; National Gallery; Burlington Arcade; Bond Street Shopping

51 BUCKINGHAM GATE, TAJ SUITES AND RESIDENCES

51 BUCKINGHAM GATE, WESTMINSTER, LONDON SW1E 6AF
Tel: 020 7769 7766 **International:** +44 (0)20 7769 7766
Web: www.condenastjohansens.com/buckinghamgate **E-mail:** reservations@51-buckinghamgate.co.uk

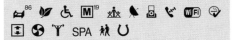

Our inspector loved: *The strikingly decorated newly appointed suites.*

Price Guide:
suites £285–£7250
prime ministers suite p.o.a.
presidential floor p.o.a

Awards/Recognition: 1 Star Michelin 2011

Location: Victoria station, 10-min walk; St Pancras, Eurostar, 5 miles; Heathrow Airport, 16 miles; Gatwick Airport, 28 miles

Attractions: Houses of Parliament; Buckingham Palace; St James Park; London Eye

This is an exceptional Victorian period townhouse hotel in the heart of Westminster just minutes from Buckingham Palace, complete with an award-winning, magical courtyard garden. The contemporary design combines subtle, state-of-the-art technology with impeccable service. The rooms are equally impressive and range from junior suites to the impressive Presidential Floor. You can indulge in the Spa at 51 exclusively offering Anne Semonin treatments or use the many other wonderful amenities including the gymnasium, saunas and steam rooms. The room service is 24 hours and nothing is too much trouble for the highly trained staff. Try the mouth watering Michelin starred Quilon for a unique and delicious dining experience. Be brave and let the chef choose for you.

Otterburn Hall

OTTERBURN, NORTHUMBERLAND NE19 1HE

Tel: 01830 520663 **International:** +44 (0)1830 520663

Web: www.condenastjohansens.com/otterburnhall **E-mail:** info@otterburnhall.com

Our inspector loved: *The unique location. This is the only hotel within Northumberland National Park.*

Price Guide:
single £81-£110
double £144-£192
suite £216

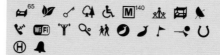

Awards/Recognition: 1 AA Rosette 2011-2012

Location: A696, 1 mile; Otterburn, 1 mile; Newcastle, 29 miles; Newcastle Airport, 24 miles

Attractions: Alnwick Castle & Gardens; Hadrian's Wall and Kielder Water; Otterburn Battle Site; Cragside

Sheltering in the secluded splendour of 500 acres comprising deer park and woodland, this most charming of mid 19th-century country house hotels is as romantic as the beautiful surrounding countryside. Grace, good taste and tranquillity reassuringly combine with the best of 21st-century comfort, convenience and great food. This is a place where time has stood still, with the stresses and pressures of modern life feeling far away. Yet the lively attractions of Newcastle are less than an hour away and historic Jedburgh, Morpeth and Hexham are even closer. Attention to detail is evident in every corner, from the luxurious bedrooms and stunning, dreamy four-poster suites to the welcoming winter log fires in the grand public rooms. In addition, mouth-watering delights are served in the award-winning Victorian restaurant whose panoramic views over the glorious grounds are stunning.

HAMBLETON HALL

HAMBLETON, OAKHAM, RUTLAND LE15 8TH
Tel: 01572 756991 **International:** +44 (0)1572 756991
Web: www.condenastjohansens.com/hambletonhall **E-mail:** hotel@hambletonhall.com

Our inspector loved: *Experiencing perfection - the welcome, the service, the accommodation, the food, the location!*

Price Guide:
single from £195
double/twin £245–£415
suite £525–£625

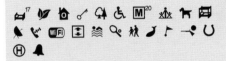

Awards/Recognition: Condé Nast Johansens Most Excellent Hotel 2011; 1 Star Michelin 2011; AA Wine Award & Overall 2010-2011; 4 AA Rosettes 2011-2012; Harden's Top 10 Restaurants 2010

Location: A606, 2 miles; Oakham, 2 miles; A1(M), 10 miles; East Midlands International Airport, 40 miles

Attractions: Hambleton Bakery; Rutland Water; Burghley House; Rockingham Castle

Originally a Victorian mansion, Hambleton Hall celebrated its 30th year as an exceptional lakeside hotel in 2010, and continues to attract acclaim for achieving near perfection. Artful blends of flowers from local hedgerows and London flower markets add splashes of colour to the bedrooms. The Croquet Pavilion a 2 bedroom suite with living and breakfast rooms is a luxurious additional option. In the Michelin-starred restaurant, chef Aaron Patterson and his brigade offer strongly seasonal menus - grouse, Scottish ceps, chanterelles, partridge and woodcock all appear when they're supposed to, accompanied by vegetables, herbs and salads from the Hall's garden. If you're feeling energetic you can embark on walks around the lake and there are opportunities for tennis, swimming, golf, cycling and sailing, otherwise you can browse for hidden treasures in Oakham's antique shops.

THE CASTLE AT TAUNTON

CASTLE GREEN, TAUNTON, SOMERSET TA1 1NF
Tel: 01823 272671 **International:** +44 (0)1823 272671
Web: www.condenastjohansens.com/castleattaunton **E-mail:** Reservations@the-castle-hotel.com

Our inspector loved: The Old World charm and contemporary style that make this a great British classic.

Price Guide: (room only)
single from £130
double from £190
garden rooms from £290

Location: Town Centre; M5 jct 25, 3 miles

Attractions: Exmoor; Somerset Levels; Wells Cathedral; Hestercombe Gardens

In the heart of the West Country, The Castle at Taunton has been welcoming travellers to explore the region's plethora of attractions since the 12th century. Run by the Chapman family for over 60 years, this former Norman fortress serves as a convivial gateway to the land of King Arthur and features 44 bedrooms, all of which are individually appointed. Gastronomes will love BRAZZ@The Castle, the fashionable brasserie overseen by Head Chef Jamie Raftery whose emphasis on regional food creates exceptional English dishes including Brixham scallops with braised pork belly and Pixford plum crumble. Alternatively, there is the intimate and sumptuous Castle Bow lounge for elegant bar food and cocktails. If you're looking for a conference or private dining then one of the Castle's five private rooms is sure to suit your style and size of party.

HOAR CROSS HALL SPA RESORT

HOAR CROSS, NEAR YOXALL, STAFFORDSHIRE DE13 8QS
Tel: 01283 575671 **International:** +44 (0)1283 575671
Web: www.condenastjohansens.com/hoarcrosshall **E-mail:** info@hoarcross.co.uk

Our inspector loved: *This excellent fully inclusive spa resort with extensive facilities and spa treatments.*

Price Guide: (including a spa treatment, breakfast, lunch and á la carte dinner)
single £172-£195
double/twin £320-£370
single/double/twin suite £230–£494

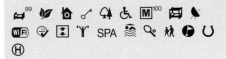

Location: A515, 2 miles; A50, 8 miles; Lichfield, 8 miles; M6 jct 12 or 15, 22 miles

Attractions: In the heart of The National Forest; Historic Lichfield

Welcome to the only stately home spa resort hotel in England and winner of England's Leading Resort, World Travel Awards 2005-2011. Surrounded by 100 acres of pretty landscaped gardens, the interior is equally beautiful with a traditional yet refreshing décor of oak panelling, tapestries, rich furnishings and paintings. The Jacobean staircase leads to the bedrooms, which all contain crown tester beds, and penthouses with private saunas and balconies; many have hot tubs overlooking the treetops. A superb à la carte menu is served in the ballroom where gilded ceilings and William Morris wallpaper set the scene. Trained experts are ready to assist with yoga, meditation, t'ai chi, Pilates, dance classes and aqua-aerobics.. The spa has sea water and hydrotherapy pools, flotation therapy baths, saunas, steam rooms, water grottos, saunariums, an aromatherapy room, 4000 sq ft gym, aerobics, yoga suites and over 100 treatments. A PGA golf academy is also available.

The Grand Hotel

KING EDWARD'S PARADE, EASTBOURNE, EAST SUSSEX BN21 4EQ

Tel: 01323 412345 **International:** +44 (0)1323 412345
Web: www.condenastjohansens.com/grandeastbourne **E-mail:** reservations@grandeastbourne.com

Our inspector loved: *This elegant seaside hotel offering a peaceful retreat, spa, fine dining and exceptional service.*

Price Guide:
double/twin £199–£350
suite £400–£555

Awards/Recognition: 2 AA Rosettes 2011-2012

Location: On the Seafront; A22, 7.5 miles; M23 jct 11, 40 miles; Gatwick Airport, 48 miles

Attractions: South Downs Way National Park; The English Wine Centre; Three Theatres; Glyndebourne Opera

A grand old dame of the Victorian period, the delightful façade of The Grand Hotel conceals reception rooms adorned with rich fabrics. Many of the 152 bedrooms have vast proportions, and each has been refurbished to include every comfort. There are numerous places in which to relax, and a good choice of restaurants and bars - the Mirabelle in particular achieves exceptional standards of fine dining. Health Club and Spa facilities include indoor and outdoor pools, gym, sauna, spa bath, steam room, snooker tables, hair salon and 8 treatment rooms featuring the Kerstin Florian skin care range and Vitaman, a specially created male grooming product. If you are seeking a peaceful retreat you'll be more than happy with the tranquil atmosphere at The Grand Hotel with its impeccably delivered standards of traditional service. Pastimes include golf at a nearby club, walks along the downs, sea fishing and visits to nearby theatres.

ASHDOWN PARK HOTEL AND COUNTRY CLUB

WYCH CROSS, FOREST ROW, EAST SUSSEX RH18 5JR
Tel: 01342 824988 **International:** +44 (0)1342 824988
Web: www.condenastjohansens.com/ashdownpark **E-mail:** reservations@ashdownpark.com

Our inspector loved: The beautiful grounds and excellent service at this historic hotel.

Price Guide:
double/twin £199-£380
suite £420–£465

Awards/Recognition: 2 AA Rosettes 2011-2012

Location: A22, 0.5 miles; M25 jct 6, 15 miles; East Grinstead, 5 miles; Gatwick Airport, 16 miles

Attractions: Ashdown Forest; Bluebell Railway; Wakehurst Place Gardens; Lingfield Park Racecourse

Set in 186 acres of East Sussex countryside, surrounded by woodland walks, free roaming deer and utter tranquillity, Ashdown Park Hotel & Country Club is ideal for those wishing to de-stress from everyday life. Whether visiting with the family or getting away with a loved one, there are 8 guest room categories to choose from; each luxuriously appointed. Relax at The Revitalise Spa and enjoy its range of pampering and relaxing treatments from the Kerstin Florian skin care range and Vitaman, a specifically created male grooming product. And enjoy the complimentary amenities of The Country Club with indoor swimming pool, steam room, sauna and 18 hole, par 3 golf course. Guests feeling particularly energetic can make use of the gym, play a game of tennis or take a jog along one of the many running trails. Complete the perfect day by dining at the 2 AA Rosette-awarded Anderida Restaurant where a resident pianist and wonderful views set the scene.

HORSTED PLACE COUNTRY HOUSE HOTEL

LITTLE HORSTED, EAST SUSSEX TN22 5TS
Tel: 01825 750581 **International:** +44 (0)1825 750581
Web: www.condenastjohansens.com/horstedplace **E-mail:** hotel@horstedplace.co.uk

Our inspector loved: The peaceful atmosphere and grand public rooms make Horsted Place feel as if you are staying in a private country house. Don't forget to play a game of croquet!

Price Guide:
mews-twin from £105
double from £145
suite from £225

Awards/Recognition: 1 AA Rosettes 2011-2012

Location: On the A26; M23 jct 10, 20 miles; Lewes, 6 miles; Gatwick, 25 miles

Attractions: Glyndebourne Opera; Sheffield Park Gardens; Bluebell Railway; East Sussex National Golf Course

The country estate of Horsted Place sits amidst the serene Sussex Downs in the south of England. Beyond the splendid Victorian gothic architecture, built in 1851, is an interior predominantly styled by the celebrated Victorian architect, Augustus Pugin. In former years the Queen and Prince Philip were frequent visitors. Guests today are invited to enjoy the excellent service offered by a committed staff. Chef Allan Garth offers a daily fixed price menu as well as the seasonal à la carte menu. The Terrace Room is an elegant and airy private function room, licensed for weddings for up to 100 guests. The smaller Morning Room and Library are ideal for boardroom-style meetings and intimate dinner parties, and the self-contained management centre offers privacy and exclusivity for business meetings in a contemporary setting.

NEWICK PARK

NEWICK, NEAR LEWES, EAST SUSSEX BN8 4SB
Tel: 01825 723633 **International:** +44 (0)1825 723633
Web: www.condenastjohansens.com/newickpark **E-mail:** bookings@newickpark.co.uk

Our inspector loved: *The beautiful countryside location and attentive yet discreet service at this award-winning hotel.*

Price Guide:
single from £125
double/twin from £165

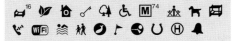

Awards/Recognition: Condé Nast Johansens Readers' Award 2011; 2 AA Rosettes 2011-2012

Location: A272, 1 mile; M23 jct 11, 18 miles; Lewes, 8 miles; Gatwick Airport, 28 miles

Attractions: Sheffield Park Garden and Wakehurst Place; Opera at Glyndebourne; Regency Brighton; Bluebell Railway

This magnificent Grade II* listed Georgian house is set in over 200 acres of beautiful parkland and landscaped gardens overlooking the Longford River and South Downs. Whilst Newick Park is situated in a convenient location near to the main road and rail routes and only 30 minutes from Gatwick Airport, the hotel maintains an atmosphere of complete tranquility and privacy. Bedrooms are decorated in a classic style featuring elegant antiques and friendly staff ensure that you receive a warm welcome. The exquisite dining room offers culinary delights carefully prepared by Head Chef, Chris Moore. The house and grounds are ideal for weddings, conferences and private parties and The Dell gardens primarily planted in Victorian times include a rare collection of Royal Ferns. Exclusive use can be arranged by appointment.

BAILIFFSCOURT HOTEL & SPA

CLIMPING, ARUNDEL, WEST SUSSEX BN17 5RW
Tel: 01903 723511 **International:** +44 (0)1903 723511
Web: www.condenastjohansens.com/bailiffscourt **E-mail:** bailiffscourt@hshotels.co.uk

Our inspector loved: The spacious bedrooms and beautiful indoor pool all make for a superbly relaxing stay.

Price Guide: (including dinner)
single from £173
double from £230
feature from £400

Step back in time at Bailiffscourt, a perfectly preserved "medieval" manor with out-buildings. Built in the 1930s using authentic material salvaged from historic old buildings, this luxurious hotel features narled 15th-century beams and gothic mullioned windows that recreate the Middle Ages. Many luxurious rooms offer four-poster beds, open log fires and beautiful views across the surrounding countryside. Menus are varied, and in summer you can eat out in the rose-clad courtyard or walled garden. The award-winning health spa features an outdoor Californian hot tub, indoor spa pool, sauna, gym, hammocks and 6 beauty rooms. 2 tennis courts and a croquet lawn complete the on-site leisure facilities, while a private pathway leads 100yds down to Climping beach, ideal for your morning walk.

Awards/Recognition: 2 AA Rosettes 2011-2012

Location: A259, 1 mile; M27 jct 1, 30 miles; Arundel, 6 miles; Gatwick Airport, 44 miles

Attractions: Arundel Castle; Goodwood Estate; Chichester Festival Theatre; Clymping Beach

OCKENDEN MANOR

OCKENDEN LANE, CUCKFIELD, WEST SUSSEX RH17 5LD
Tel: 01444 416111 **International:** +44 (0)1444 416111
Web: www.condenastjohansens.com/ockendenmanor **E-mail:** ockenden@hshotels.co.uk

Our inspector loved: *The newly refurbished restaurant and excitement surrounding the soon-to-be-open spa.*

Price Guide:
single from £110
double £183–£332
suite £299–£376

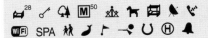

Awards/Recognition: 1 Star Michelin 2011;
3 AA Rosettes 2011-2012

Location: A272, 0.5 mile; M23 jct 10, 4 miles;
Haywards Heath, 2 miles; Gatwick Airport,
18 miles

Attractions: Wakehurst and Nymans Gardens;
Glyndebourne Opera; Regency Brighton;
Bluebell Railway

History and character abound in this enchanting Elizabethan manor house hotel, which was first recorded in 1520, and lies tucked away in one of the prettiest Tudor villages in the country, ideal for exploring Sussex and Kent. From the minute you step through its welcoming doors, you're swept away by warm hospitality and culinary delights. 28 distinctive bedrooms and suites offer an array of fascinating features: climb your own private staircase to Elizabeth, indulge in a Victorian-style bath in Hugh, or enjoy the huge four-poster bed in Charles, to name but a few. The romantic restaurant, with its sweeping views across the garden and beyond, is the perfect setting to enjoy innovative, Michelin-Starred cuisine and an inspired wine list. Guests in need of serious pampering will adore the new spa, which is fed by its own underground spring and shares the manor's 9 acres of peaceful gardens and parkland with its breathtaking views across the South Downs.

Felbridge Hotel & Spa

LONDON ROAD, EAST GRINSTEAD, WEST SUSSEX RH19 2BH
Tel: 01342 337700 **International:** +44 (0)1342 337700
Web: www.condenastjohansens.com/felbridgehotel **E-mail:** sales@felbridgehotel.co.uk

Our inspector loved: The comfortable bedrooms and leisure facilities at this stylish hotel.

Price Guide:
single £89-£170
double £99-£180
suite £189-£310

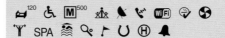

Felbridge Hotel & Spa is a sophisticated property in the South of England with an elegant interior of contemporary design beyond the immaculate and traditional exterior. Well-styled bedrooms in fresh neutral tones range from standard doubles to luxury junior suites, and welcome additions include the Bay Tree Restaurant and Anise fine dining restaurant. The chic QUBE Bar brings a touch of glamour to the proceedings! Luxuriate in a treatment at the Chakra Spa - sheer indulgence. The hotel has gone from strength to strength in the last year and at 86%, it is the AA's top rated 4 Black Star hotel in the South East. A deserved accolade you will no doubt agree with, as it cleverly makes the most of its calm, relaxing atmosphere and location just 10 minutes from Gatwick Airport.

Awards/Recognition: 2 AA Rosettes 2011-2012

Location: On the A22; M23 jct 10, 7 miles; M25 jct 6, 9 miles; Gatwick Airport, 7 miles

Attractions: Wakehurst Place Gardens; Hever Castle; Chartwell, Churchill's Home; Royal Tunbridge Wells

Park House Hotel & PH$_2$O Spa

BEPTON, MIDHURST, WEST SUSSEX GU29 0JB
Tel: 01730 819 000 **International:** +44 (0)1730 819 000
Web: www.condenastjohansens.com/parkhousehotel **E-mail:** reservations@parkhousehotel.com

Our inspector loved: This small luxury hotel has everything from a fabulous spa to luxurious bedrooms and fine cuisine.

Price Guide:
single £135
double £135-£224
suite £240-£360

Location: Gatwick Airport, 37 miles; Heathrow Airport, 45 miles; A3, 12 miles; A27, 13 miles

Attractions: Weald and Downland Open Air Museum; Petworth House; Goodwood Racecourse and Estate; Cowdray Ruins

Park House Hotel is a quintessential English country house hotel located in 10 acres of South Downs National Park, an area of outstanding natural beauty, close to the historic market town of Midhurst. Family run and family friendly, this home from home hotel is warm and welcoming with a designer touch. Most guest rooms look out to stunning views of the surrounding rose garden, ponds, croquet and bowls lawns, golf course and swimming pool. And within these pretty grounds are 3 private cottages that can be reserved for exclusive use. 2 have a kitchen, however, the seasonal, locally sourced dishes at the hotel's restaurant are irresistible and its menu always features English favourites. A restored Sussex barn, located next to the main house, is a superb venue for a party, business meeting or wedding reception, and let's not forget the new PH$_2$O spa, a state-of-the-art therapeutic, fitness and luxury facility offering a variety of packages and services.

THE SPREAD EAGLE HOTEL & SPA

SOUTH STREET, MIDHURST, WEST SUSSEX GU29 9NH
Tel: 01730 816911 **International:** +44 (0)1730 816911
Web: www.condenastjohansens.com/spreadeaglemidhurst **E-mail:** spreadeagle@hshotels.co.uk

Our inspector loved: The perfect place for discovering the Sussex countryside, The hotel is steeped in history and full of character.

Price Guide: (including dinner)
single from £125-£390
double from £190-£390
suites from £290

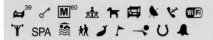

Awards/Recognition: 2 AA Rosettes 2011-2012

Location: Town Centre; Just off A272/286, 0.2 miles; M25 jct 9, 31 miles; Gatwick Airport, 38 miles

Attractions: Petworth House; Cowdray Park; Goodwood House and Estate; Chichester Cathedral; West Dean Gardens

The historic Spread Eagle Hotel is one of England's oldest hotels, dating from 1430 and rich in charm and period features cleverly mixed with modern luxuries. This West Sussex hotel is perfect for a luxury spa break: it boasts an outstanding modern Spa – with an impressive vaulted glass ceiling and plenty of wet areas. In the restaurant Nathan Marshall creates a modern classic menu using seasonal flavours and plenty of local produce. The bedrooms are delightful, many with antiques and some with four-poster beds. The White Room contains a 'secret passage' and is said to have been used by smugglers in their attempt to evade the King's men. With easy access to Sussex and the South Downs, this is a great area to explore whether walking, shopping or enjoying any number of outdoor activities, after which a cream tea at the Spread Eagle will be well deserved. Childrens' high-teas can be arranged and well-behaved dogs are allowed in some bedrooms.

GRAVETYE MANOR

VOWELS LANE, NEAR WEST HOATHLY, WEST SUSSEX RH19 4LJ
Tel: 01342 810567 **International:** +44 (0)1342 810567
Web: www.condenastjohansens.com/gravetyemanor **E-mail:** info@gravetyemanor.co.uk

Our inspector loved: *The relaxing atmosphere, discreet service and beautiful gardens.*

Price Guide:
standard £240-£290
superior £280-£315
de luxe £355-£430

Awards/Recognition: 3 AA Rosettes 2011-2012

Location: East Grinstead station, 4 miles; Gatwick Airport, 13 miles; M25 jct 6, 14 miles

Attractions: Royal Ashdown golf Course; Wakehurst Place; Hever Castle; Standen (NT)

Drive a mile through private Sussex woods to find this enchanting Elizabethan manor house hotel steeped in history. Friendly and unstuffy, with a welcoming atmosphere, Gravetye is surrounded by 35 acres of renowned gardens with fine stone walls. This was the former home of gardener and pioneer William Robinson until 1935, and it was here that he realised many of his ideals for the creation of The English Natural Garden. The house and its interiors more than live up to this standard with 17 beautifully appointed rooms ranging from standard to de luxe. In the intimate, oak-panelled restaurant enjoy the "modern British" cuisine of highly acclaimed Chef Rupert Gleadow. Rupert prides himself on the use of locally sourced organic produce where possible, with much grown on Gravetye's own garden and local farms. Run by a young team of dedicated professionals, the hotel's service is impeccable, and it can host meetings, special events and civil wedding ceremonies.

NAILCOTE HALL

NAILCOTE LANE, BERKSWELL, NEAR SOLIHULL, WARWICKSHIRE CV7 7DE
Tel: 02476 466174 **International:** +44 (0)2476 466174
Web: www.condenastjohansens.com/nailcotehall **E-mail:** info@nailcotehall.co.uk

Our inspector loved: *The pretty and challenging Par 3 golf course matched by comfortable hospitality.*

Price Guide:
single £185
double/twin £200
suite £200–£305

Located in the heart of England, Nailcote Hall is a charming hotel that dates back to Elizabethan times. Built in 1640, Oliver Cromwell and his troops used this now fully restored country house hotel during the Civil War. The intimate Tudor surrounds of the Oak Room restaurant, the luxury accommodation and impressive leisure facilities are all enticing features. These include a Roman style swimming pool, gym, solarium and steam room, outside all-weather tennis courts, pétanque, croquet, a challenging 9-hole par-3 golf course and putting green - host to the "British Par 3 Championship". Nailcote Hall is within 15 minutes' drive of the castle towns of Kenilworth and Warwick, Coventry Cathedral, Birmingham International Airport/Station and the NEC.

Location: A452, 2 miles; M42 jct 5, 7 miles; Balsall Common, 3 miles; Birmingham International, 9 miles

Attractions: Warwick Castle; Kenilworth Castle; Coventry Cathedral; Royal Leamington Spa; Stratford-Upon-Avon

HAMPTON MANOR

SHADOWBROOK LANE, HAMPTON-IN-ARDEN, SOLIHULL, WARWICKSHIRE B92 0EN
Tel: 01675 446080 **International:** +44 (0)1675 446080
Web: www.condenastjohansens.com/hamptonmanor **E-mail:** info@hamptonmanor.eu

Our inspector loved: The chic style of this hidden away hotel, and Peels Restaurant's mouthwatering gourmet menu.

Price Guide:
single from £156
double £172-£240
suite £282-£360

Location: M42, 2 miles; B4438, 1 miles; A45, 1.5 miles; Birmingham NEC, 3 miles; Birmingham International Airport, 3 miles

Attractions: NEC; Stratford-upon-Avon; Warwick Castle; Forest of Arden Country Club

This beautiful 19th-century manor house is a small, luxurious hotel offering a blend of traditional charm and contemporary chic. Set in 45 acres, this Midlands hotel is surprisingly just minutes from Birmingham's airport, motorways and rail links. The individual bedrooms in the original manor house include feature rooms and suites furnished by designer John Reeves. All of the stylish finishes blend sensitively with the essence of each room, whether it be a huge tub at the end of the bed, gorgeous garden views or quirky touches. Peel's fine dining restaurant is located in the courtyard and is overlooked by the clocktower. Acclaimed Chef Martyn Pearn uses his experience, attention to detail, passion for perfectly cooked food and the best ingredients to create sophisticated, elegant dishes. For cocktails and more informal dining head to Peel's Bar, set behind the arches of the old coach house. The Manor is available for meetings, private dining, weddings and celebrations.

113

Welcombe Hotel Spa & Golf Club

WARWICK ROAD, STRATFORD-UPON-AVON, WARWICKSHIRE CV37 0NR
Tel: 01789 295252 **International:** +44 (0)1789 295252
Web: www.condenastjohansens.com/welcombe **E-mail:** welcombe.sales@menzieshotels.co.uk

Our inspector loved: *The impressive spa with outdoor vitality pool and thermal experience rooms.*

Price Guide:
single from £99
double from £110
executive from £150

Awards/Recognition: 2 AA Rosettes 2011-2012

Location: Stratford-Upon-Avon, 1.6 miles; A439, 3 miles; M40 jct 15, 6 miles; Warwick, 8 miles

Attractions: Warwick Castle; The Cotswolds; Royal Shakespeare Company Theatre; Shakespeare's Birthplace

Known as one of the UK's top country house hotels, this stunning luxury retreat offers some of the finest leisure facilities in the heart of England. Whether you are looking for a spa break, golfing holiday or romantic getaway, the Jacobean-style Welcombe is irresistible. Its traditional charm, oak panelled lounge, ornate restaurant and magnificent four-poster suites superbly blend with the modern décor of the garden rooms and spa. When it comes to cuisine, the emphasis is on pleasure. Fine, seasonal produce is combined to create clean, satisfying flavours for intimate diners or banquets of up to 120. With beautiful Italian gardens overlooking rolling countryside, this is also a wonderfully romantic wedding location. Brides-to be should take full advantage of the spa's blissful thermal experience rooms and luxurious treatments while nervous grooms can test their skills on the championship 18-hole golf course!

LUCKNAM PARK HOTEL & SPA

COLERNE, CHIPPENHAM, WILTSHIRE SN14 8AZ
Tel: 01225 742777 **International:** +44 (0)1225 742777
Web: www.condenastjohansens.com/lucknampark **E-mail:** reservations@lucknampark.co.uk

Our inspector loved: The mix of old and modern from the cutting edge spa to the beauty and elegance of the palladian mansion house.

Price Guide: (room only)
single/double/twin from £330
suite from £725

Awards/Recognition: Condé Nast Johansens Most Excellent Spa 2011; 1 Star Michelin 2011; Relais & Châteaux; 3 AA Rosettes 2011-2012

Location: A420, 1.5 miles; M4 jct 18, 9 miles; Bristol, 20 miles

Attractions: Bath; Lacock; Castle Combe; Westonbirt Arboretum; Longleat

Lucknam Park country house hotel in Bath is a spectacular Palladian mansion set within a 500-acre private estate six miles from the historic city of Bath. A majestic 5 star luxury hotel, boasting the award winning restaurant The Park (we recommend you book in advance) that delivers both elegant sophistication and the warm comfort of an English country house. The acclaimed spa, is exceptional, with its clean lines of natural materials fused with floor to ceiling windows lends itself to total relaxation. Features include a 20-metre heated pool, indoor-outdoor hydrotherapy pool, thermal cabins and nine state-of-the-art treatment rooms using products from Anne Semonin and Carita, Paris. Here, there is also a stylish and contemporary Brasserie featuring an open kitchen. For the more energetic there is an Equestrian Centre, two floodlit tennis courts, a five-a-side football pitch, croquet lawn and mountain bikes.

WHATLEY MANOR

EASTON GREY, MALMESBURY, WILTSHIRE SN16 0RB
Tel: 01666 822888 **International:** +44 (0)1666 822888
Web: www.condenastjohansens.com/whatley **E-mail:** reservations@whatleymanor.com

Our inspector loved: The peace, tranquility and exceptional service combined with a welcoming yet luxurious atmosphere make this a very special place to stay.

Price Guide: (including full English breakfast, daily newspaper, use of spa facilities and 10% discretionary service charge)
standard from £305
superior/deluxe £375-£515
suite £665-£865

Looking to book a spa break, enjoy an award-winning gastronomic experience or simply relax in luxurious surroundings. Then this beautifully designed, stylish and sophisticated retreat nestling in 12 acres of Wiltshire countryside on the doorstep to the Cotswolds is for you. Very careful attention to detail is evident throughout the 15 bedrooms and 8 suites furnished with Italian furniture and handmade French wallpaper each entirely individual. The atmosphere is welcoming and feels more like a family owned country home. There are two gastronomic experiences on offer the Michelin two-starred restaurant "The Dining Room" and the more informal brasserie, "Le Mazot" with its refreshingly alternative Swiss interior. The highly acclaimed spa, Aquarias, includes one of the largest hydrotherapy pools in the UK and a La Prairie "Art of Beauty" Centre. A private cinema accommodates up to 40 people and the 12 acres of gardens have 26 distinct areas for you to explore.

Awards/Recognition: 2 Star Michelin 2011; 4 AA Rosettes 2011-2012; Relais & Châteaux

Location: Off the B4040; A429, 3 miles; M4 jct 17, 8 miles; London, 75-min train

Attractions: The Cotswolds; Bath; Malmesbury Abbey & Gardens; Tetbury; Westonbirt Arboretum

DORMY HOUSE

WILLERSEY HILL, BROADWAY, WORCESTERSHIRE WR12 7LF
Tel: 01386 852711 **International:** +44 (0)1386 852711
Web: www.condenastjohansens.com/dormyhouse **E-mail:** reservations@dormyhouse.co.uk

Our inspector loved: The picturesque Cotswold location, sitting on the top of Fish Hill with views over the Vale of Evesham.

Price Guide:
single from £130
double/twin from £190
suite from £210

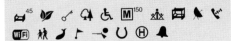

Awards/Recognition: 2 AA Rosettes 2011-2012

Location: A44, ¼ mile; Broadway, 3 miles; M40 jct 8 or 15, 25 miles; Birmingham International, 41 miles

Attractions: Cotswolds; Cheltenham; Stratford-upon-Avon; Hidcote Manor; Kiftsgate Gardens

A charming home from home with more than a dash of panache, Dormy House is a tastefully converted farmhouse that dates back to the 17th century in the heart of the fairytale Cotswolds. A haven of luxury for anyone who loves to relax, indulge and enjoy life. Behind its mellow stone walls is a welcoming, intimate warmth, with an interior filled with deep comfy sofas, cosy leather armchairs, and a refreshing, unstuffy atmosphere of a lived-in home where nothing is too much trouble. Laid-back elegance is the premise of the 45 individually designed bedrooms and suites. Their comfort is typified by crisp bed linen and plump pillows, and unique character is created by a harmonious mix of traditional English furniture and rich fabrics. Work on your well-being in the Moroccan sauna and steam room, take on the challenge of the hotel's 9-hole putting green and, above all, don't miss eating in the delightful, 2 Rosette-awarded Dining Room or the Barn Owl Brasserie.

RUDDING PARK HOTEL, SPA & GOLF

FOLLIFOOT, HARROGATE, NORTH YORKSHIRE HG3 1JH

Tel: 01423 871 350 **International:** +44 (0)1423 871 350
Web: www.condenastjohansens.com/ruddingpark **E-mail:** sales@ruddingpark.com

Rudding Park is an imposing Grade 1 listed Regency house with 21st-century comforts located 2½ miles south of Harrogate, within easy reach of Leeds and York. Surrounded by secluded gardens and parkland with a challenging championship golf course and golf academy, this beautiful house is a wonderful getaway for a romantic weekend, pamper days in a luxury spa or fine dining in the stunning Clocktower restaurant. Comfortable guest rooms feature modern fabrics and tasteful colours. An AA 4 red star hotel with a welcoming, contemporary feel, this is a special place to indulge in all that is good about Yorkshire. A deserved winner of a multitude of awards including No. 1 Best UK Hotel at TripAdvisor Travellers' Choice Awards 2010 and 2011.

Our inspector loved: The contemporary new bedrooms and the helpful and attentive staff.

Price Guide:
single £105-£322
double £126-£343
suite from £245

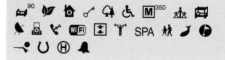

Awards/Recognition: 2 AA Rosettes 2011-2012

Location: Harrogate, 2.5 miles; A1M, 6 miles; Leeds, 17 miles; Leeds Bradford Airport, 30-min drive

Attractions: Harlow Carr; Yorkshire Dales; Harewood House; Newby Hall

SIMONSTONE HALL

HAWES, NORTH YORKSHIRE DL8 3LY
Tel: 01969 667255 **International:** +44 (0)1969 667255
Web: www.condenastjohansens.com/simonstonehall **E-mail:** enquiries@simonstonehall.com

Our inspector loved: *The beautiful location and the stunning views across Upper Wensleydale.*

Price Guide:
single £110–£150
double/twin £155–£205

Location: A684, 1.5 miles; Hawes, 1.5 miles; M6 jct 37, 30-min drive; A1M, 40-min drive

Attractions: Hardraw Force; Wensleydale Creamery Cheese Factory; Yorkshire Dales; Bolton Castle

Simonstone Hall is one of the finest Yorkshire Dales hotels with wonderful views of Wensleydale. A former 18th-century hunting lodge the Hall has been lovingly restored and furnished with antiques to create a romantic hotel perfect for wedding receptions and is an idyllic, memorable retreat. Standing in a beautiful setting adjacent to 4,000 acres of grouse moors and upland grazing, many of the building's period features have been retained such as the panelled dining room, mahogany staircase with ancestral stained glass windows and a lounge with ornamental ceilings. The bedrooms are of a high standard, 4 offer four-poster comfort and 2 have sleigh beds. The formal dining room, with its stunning views across Upper Wensleydale, serves an à la carte menu composed of the freshest local produce along with an excellent wine list to complement any dish. Warm, informal dining and traditional cuisine can be enjoyed in The Pub and The Brasserie.

SCOT

City of Derry

Coleraine

A37

A2

Londonderry

N14

A26

A44

A6

A29

M2

A36

Lar

A505

M2

N15

A32

A5

Belfast

A46

A4

A5

A29

Belfast

M1

A1

A20

Ballina

Sligo

A4

Armagh

A7

N26

N17

N4

A28

A24

N5

129

N16

Cavan

A2

Newry

A1

N15

N3

Dundalk

Knock International

N5

Longford

M1

128

N17

N4

Drogheda

N2

125

N6

Athlone

M4

Dublin

Galway

126

M4

Dublin

N18

N7

N7

Dun Laoghaire

130

Shannon

122

Shannon

M7

N11

Limerick

N7

N9

N24

Kilkenny

Tralee

N21

N10

N9

N30

N20

N9

Wexford

Killarney

127

N24

N25

N22

N8

Waterford

Cork

N25

Kenmare

Cork

123

124

Ireland

For further information on
Ireland, please contact:

The Irish Tourist Board
(Bord Fáilte Éireann)
Tel: 0808 234 2009
www.discoverireland.com

Tourism Ireland
Tel: +353 (0)1476 3400
www.tourismireland.com

Irish Georgian Society
74 Merrion Square
Dublin 2
Tel: +353 (0)1676 7053
www.ige.ie

Irish Ferries
Tel: 0818 300400
www.irishferries.com

The Guinness Brewery
Tel: +353 (0)1408 4800
www.guinness-storehouse.com

Aer Lingus
Tel: +353 (0)818 365000
www.aerlingus.com

or see **pages 157-160** for details of local historic
houses, castles and gardens to visit during your stay.

For additional places to stay in Ireland, turn to
pages 151-155 where a listing of our Recommended
Small Hotels, Inns & Restaurants can be found.

The g Hotel, Galway, Ireland – p126

DROMOLAND CASTLE

NEWMARKET-ON-FERGUS, CO CLARE
Tel: 00 353 61368144
Web: www.condenastjohansens.com/dromolandcastle **E-mail:** sales@dromoland.ie

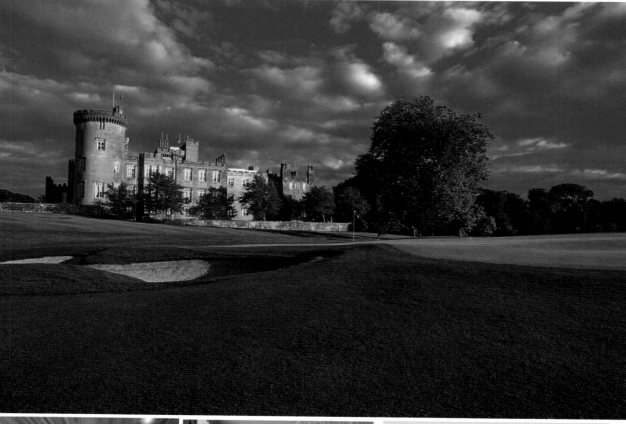

Our inspector loved: The overwhelming sense of history, with style and exemplary service, in abundance.

Price Guide: (euro, room only)
single/double €225–€573
suite €471–€955

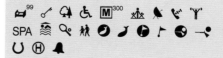

Location: N18, 3 miles; Limerick, 19 miles; Shannon Airport, 8 miles

Attractions: Dramatic West Coast; The Cliffs of Moher & The Buren region; Galway City & The Aran Islands; Bunratty Castle & Folk Park; King Johns Castle

Arriving at this majestic hotel is like stepping into a fairy tale. Dromoland Castle is one of the most impressive and magical castle hotels in Ireland and dates all the way back to the 5th century, when it was the home of Gaelic royalty. The baronial sumptuousness of the interior design befits its history, and is wonderfully combined with contemporary conveniences. Attentive staff provide service fit for a king! There is no doubt that you will feel pampered and relaxed. Sink into a comfy chair and read a good book by the fireside before heading off to the spa, an intimate haven within the heart of the castle, complete with indoor pool and sauna. Delicious dishes inspired by seasonal produce and Irish tradition are served in restaurant; you can even have a luxury picnic basket prepared. A Member of the Dromoland Collection.

CASTLEMARTYR RESORT

CASTLEMARTYR, CO CORK
Tel: 00 353 21 4219000
Web: www.condenastjohansens.com/castlemartyr **E-mail:** reception@castlemartyrresort.ie

Our inspector loved: The attention to detail, locally produced ingredients for great dishes and a relaxing spa.

Price Guide: (euro)
single €185-€375
double €199-€375
suite €354-€875

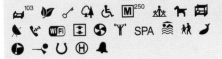

Location: Midleton, 6 miles; Cork City, 18 miles; Cork Airport, 22 miles; Dungarven, 27 miles

Attractions: Kinsale; Titanic Trail, Cobh; Old Jameson Distillery; Fota Wild Life Park; English Market

Past a gently meandering river, you will come upon the 5 star luxury Castlemartyr Resort, an exquisite hotel that dates back to the 17th-century and today, exudes luxury and elegance complemented by a high standard of service. The opulent bedrooms are impeccably styled with a handsome combination of antiques, lavish fabrics and every modern amenity. The spa is unlike any other: a spacious and light idyll where you can leave your worries behind and indulge in a rejuvenating treatment. Do not miss the pleasure of the restaurant's innovative cuisine! The ingredients are fresh, locally produced and of exceptional quality. During the day, explore the countless delights of this large country estate, with its rolling hills, mature woodlands, tranquil lake teeming with wildlife and stunning golf course. Take a stroll, enjoy a game of croquet, or simply relax and admire your surroundings. A Member of the Dromoland Collection.

Fota Island Hotel & Spa

FOTA ISLAND RESORT, FOTA ISLAND, CO CORK
Tel: 00 353 21 488 3700 **International:** +44 (0)0 353 21 488 3700
Web: www.condenastjohansens.com/fotaisland **E-mail:** reservations@fotaisland.ie

Our inspector loved: *The opportunity to be totally indulged by the experts!*

Price Guide: (euro)
single from €125
double from €140
junior suite from €235

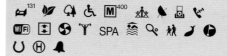

Indulge yourself with 5 star luxury at this exceptional Cork hotel and resort, either by playing golf on one of its 3 challenging championship golf courses or unwinding in the opulent spa. The contemporary styled bedrooms and suites are spacious and supremely comfortable, decorated in warm, subtle shades. All have air conditioning, flat-screen TVs and bathrooms featuring rainforest showers, while some boast balconies and stunning views across the woodlands and parkland. Many services such as babysitting and laundry are available upon request. Nestling within one of the most outstanding natural settings on the Irish coast, it would be hard not to relax at the spa, complete with full fitness suite, indoor pool and 18 treatment rooms. Once you've worked out or worked your way around the golf courses, enjoy dinner at the tempting selection of restaurants. Exclusive golf lodges set around the resort provide total privacy. Events and wedding packages can also be arranged.

Location: Cobh 5-min drive; Cork, 10-min drive; Kinsale 35-min drive Cork International Airport, 20-min drive

Attractions: City of Cork; Cork Harbour; Fota Wildlife Park; Fota House & Gardens

CASHEL HOUSE

CASHEL, CONNEMARA, CO GALWAY
Tel: 00 353 95 31001
Web: www.condenastjohansens.com/cashelhouse **E-mail:** res@cashel-house-hotel.com

Our inspector loved: This totally unspoilt oasis, surrounded by beautiful gardens.

Price Guide: (euro)
single €105–€270
double/twin €210–€350
suite €300–€395

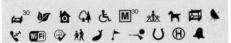

Awards/Recognition: Condé Nast Johansens Best Value for Money 2010; 2 AA Rosettes 2011-2012

Location: N59, 60km; Galway, 65km; Galway Airport, 70km

Attractions: Connemara National Park; Stud Farm; Delightful Gardens and Garden School; Aran and Inish Boffin Islands; Kylemore Abbey Victorian Walled Gardens

Surrounded by exotic flowering gardens and woodland walks at the head of Cashel Bay, this pretty hotel was built in 1840 for Captain Thomas Hazel, an English landowner, by the owners' great, great grandfather. Today, the McEvilly family welcome you to their tastefully furnished home where turf and log fires invite you to relax and comfortable bedrooms and suites offer hill or garden views. In the dining room, Chef Ray Doorley oversees the ever-changing menu of imaginative dishes featuring local seafood, lamb, beef, game and home-grown vegetables alongside a carefully chosen wine list. Outside, the stunning surrounds offer a plethora of activities such as golf, fishing, bird watching, hill walking and mountain hiking. And furthermore, Cashel House has its very own beach, on-site stud farm and 50 acres of award-winning gardens where various 2 and 3-day gardening courses, including garden design, restoration, vegetable, herb and fruit growing, take place.

THE G HOTEL

WELLPARK, GALWAY, CO GALWAY
Tel: 00 353 91 865 200
Web: www.condenastjohansens.com/theghotel **E-mail:** reservetheg@theg.ie

Our inspector loved: The "wow" factor in every aspect of this impressive hotel and spa.

Price Guide: (euro)
single from €125
double from €140
suite from €300

SPA

Located in the heart of Galway, The g is a 5 star luxury hotel that effortlessly combines the best of traditional Irish hospitality with stunning contemporary design, offering you a truly unforgettable experience. The hotel's glamorous interiors were created by remarkable milliner, Philip Treacy, with an emphasis on harmonious opulence that is inspired by the landscape and seashores of Galway. Make time to visit the spa, which is situated over 2 floors of the hotel and offers a wide range of ESPA treatments within a distinctively relaxing space that is simply perfect for pampering and indulging yourself. However, you may never want to leave your beautiful bedroom! Each is spacious, comfortable and has amazing cutting-edge in-room entertainment. Delicious Irish cuisine is cooked to perfection and served in a dazzling dining room, Matz at the g that combines lavish purple velvet banqueting with jewel-coloured Andrew Martin chairs.

Awards/Recognition: Top 3 hotels in the world for design & ambience, Condé Nast Traveller Gold List 2009; "Best Chef in Galway" Irish Restaurant Awards 2010

Location: City Centre, 1 km; Galway Airport, 15-min drive; Shannon Airport, 1-hour drive; Knock Airport, 75-mins drive; Dublin Airport, 2-hours drive

Attractions: Spanish Arch; Galway Cathedral; Connemara National Park; Cliffs of Moher; Aran Islands

CAHERNANE HOUSE HOTEL

MUCKROSS ROAD, KILLARNEY, CO KERRY
Tel: 00 353 64 6631895
Web: www.condenastjohansens.com/cahernane **E-mail:** info@cahernane.com

Our inspector loved: *The individual personality and warm hospitality at all times.*

Price Guide: (euro)
single from €90
double from €130
suite from €200

Awards/Recognition: 2 AA Rosette 2011-2012

Location: Killarney, 1 mile; Kerry Airport, 14 miles

Attractions: Ring of Kerry; Muckross House; Killarney Golf club; Killarney National Park

A shady tunnel of greenery frames the ¼ mile long drive to this welcoming house that dates back to the 17th-century, where time seems to move at a wonderfully sedate pace. The former home to the Earls of Pembroke it stands in gorgeous parklands on the edge of Killarney's National Park, Co Kerry. You'll find the Browne family pride themselves on their hospitality and will be keen to ensure you make the most of your stay. Bedrooms have plenty of individual personality and the suites are enhanced with beautiful antiques. Recipient of numerous awards, Herbert Room restaurant offers menus by chef David Norris, or you can eat more informally in the Cellar Bar, home to an impressive stock of wines. There's tennis and croquet or simply enjoy garden walks and views of the National Parks untamed beauty.

Ashford Castle

CONG, CO MAYO
Tel: 00 353 94 95 46003
Web: www.condenastjohansens.com/ashfordcastle **E-mail:** ashford@ashford.ie

Our inspector loved: The wonderful staff whose welcoming smiles are as wide as the stunning views!

Price Guide: (euro, room only)
single/twin/double from €175
stateroom/suite from €450

SPA

Awards/Recognition: Condé Nast Traveller Readers Choice - Number 1 Resort hotel in Europe 2010; Condé Nast Johansens Most Excellent Waterside Hotel 2009

Location: N84, 9km; Galway City, 42km; Galway Airport, 44km; Shannon Airport, 125km; Dublin Airport, 254km

Attractions: Connemara Loop; Connemara National Park; Westport: Ceidhe Fields; Leenane

This 13th-century castle stands within 350 acres of stunning estate and is the former home of Lord Ardilaun and the Guinness family. It became a luxurious hotel in 1939 and is now a veritable playground for fishing, nature and golf enthusiasts. Food lovers will also appreciate the exceptional cuisine. The Chef's creativity and inspirational use of local, seasonal and organic ingredients offer a range of dining options to suit all occasions. Choose from the 5-course table d'hôte evening menu in the George V restaurant, adorned with 11 Waterford crystal chandeliers, or the informal bistro-style à la carte menu at Cullen's at the Cottage. A daily snack menu is served in the Drawing Room and a 24-hour in-room dining service is also available. Relax after dinner to nightly entertainment, and enjoy the activities and facilities including falconry, clay pigeon shooting, health centre and treatment rooms. Boat trips can be arranged on Lough Corrib.

KNOCKRANNY HOUSE HOTEL & SPA

WESTPORT, CO MAYO
Tel: 00 353 98 28600
Web: www.condenastjohansens.com/knockranny **E-mail:** info@khh.ie

Our inspector loved: *The superb service, delicious menus, highly commended wine list and a spa!*

Price Guide: (euro)
single from €105
double/twin from €140
suite from €210

Awards/Recognition: Condé Nast Johansens/ Taittinger Wine List Award 2011; 2 AA Rosette 2011-2012; "La Fougere"'Best Restaurant in Connaught 2011; Head Chef-Seamus Commons, Best Chef in Connaught 2011

Location: Just off the N5; Town Centre 10-min walk; Train & Bus Station 15-min walk; Knock Airport, 45-mins drive

Attractions: Westport House Estate; Great Western Greenway cycle & walkway: Croagh Patrick Mountain; Clewbay & Clare Island

Rising into view against Croagh Patrick Mountain this Victorian house with luxury spa evokes an image of a bygone era. Set in secluded grounds in Westport, Co Mayo, Knockranny is comfortable and welcoming. With a reputation as one of Ireland's finest hotels since 1997, you have a wide choice of bedrooms with courtyard or mountain views including Grand De Luxe - De Luxe - Master Suites and Executive Suites. The new rooms are very spacious and feature king-size beds, 32" LCD TVs, surround-sound systems, free broadband internet access, oversized bathrooms with spa bath as standard. Antique furniture features throughout the hotel and the conservatory and library look out onto magnificent scenery. You can enjoy contemporary Irish cuisine and fish dishes in the restaurant. Spa Salveo features a vitality pool, a serail mud chamber and 12 treatment rooms.

THE RITZ-CARLTON, POWERSCOURT

POWERSCOURT ESTATE, ENNISKERRY, CO WICKLOW

Tel: 00 353 1 274 8888

Web: www.condenastjohansens.com/ritzcarlton **E-mail:** powerscourtreservations@ritzcarlton.com

Our inspector loved: The "nothing is too difficult" attitude, stunning spa and lots of style!

Price Guide: (euro)
deluxe from €235
superior from €245
garden view suite from €275
mountain view suite from €285

Location: Dublin Airport, 45-min drive; Dublin City Centre, 30-min drive; Glendalough, 40-min drive; Dun Laoghaire Ferry Port, 25-min drive

Attractions: Powerscourt House & Gardens; Glendalough; Dublin City Centre; Trinity College

Surrounded by the serene woodlands, gentle green hills and sparkling lakes of Powerscourt Estate, with glorious views of the County Wicklow countryside, this sumptuous country estate beckons with an irresistible blend of luxurious country living and impeccable service, and yet cosmopolitan Dublin is only half an hour away. The bedrooms and suites are generously sized and decorated in a casually elegant style; many offer floor-to-ceiling windows, panoramic views and terraces. Dining is a delight: choose between Gordon Ramsay at Powerscourt, where the professional team creates culinary delights and the more casual Sugar Loaf Lounge, which also houses a welcoming bar. For ultimate relaxation, the peaceful ESPA treats guests to absolute luxury with 21 treatment rooms, a 20-metre Swarovski crystal-lit pool, fitness suite and state-of-the-art thermal suite. The stunning 36-hole championship golf complex is located only a few steps from the hotel.

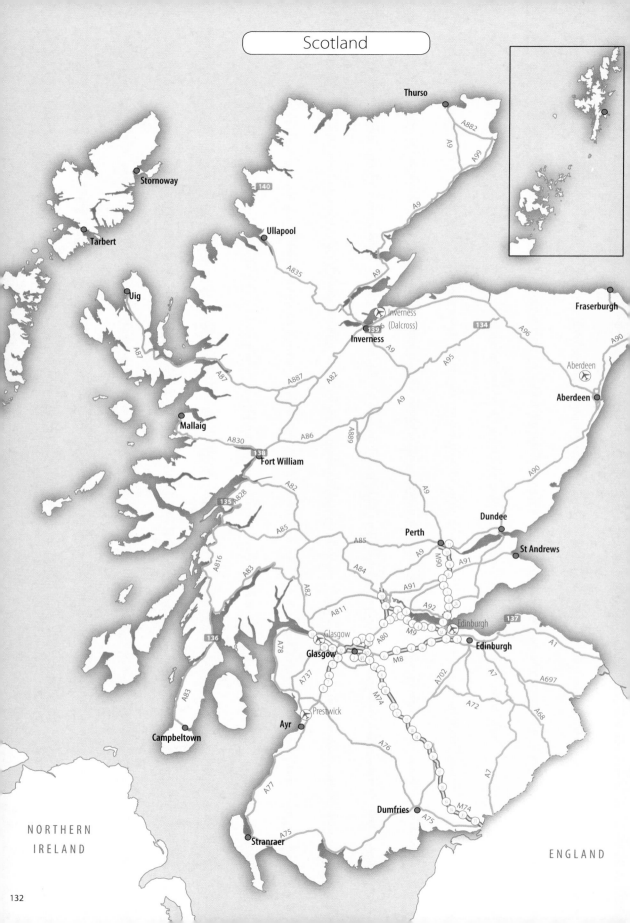

Scotland

Thurso

A882

A9

A99

Stornoway

140

A9

Ullapool

A835

A9

Fraserburgh

Inverness (Dalcross)

134

A96

A90

139

Inverness

A9

A95

Aberdeen

Uig

A887

A82

A9

Aberdeen

A87

A887

A86

A889

Mallaig

A830

A86

A889

138 Fort William

A90

135 A828

A82

A85

A82

A85

Perth

Dundee

A816

A83

A85

A84

A91

St Andrews

A82

A811

A91

A92

136

Glasgow

A80

M9

Edinburgh

137

A78

Glasgow

M8

Edinburgh

A1

A737

A702

A7

A697

Prestwick

M74

A72

Ayr

A68

Campbeltown

A76

A7

A77

Dumfries

M74

Stranraer

A75

A75

NORTHERN

IRELAND

ENGLAND

Scotland

Inverlochy Castle, Highland, Scotland – p138

For further information on Scotland, please contact:

Visit Scotland
Ocean Point 1,
94 Ocean Drive
Edinburgh EH6 6JH
Tel: 0845 22 55 121
www.visitscotland.com

Greater Glasgow & Clyde Valley Tourist Board
11 George Square
Glasgow G2 1DY
Tel: +44 (0)141 566 0800
www.seeglasgow.com

Edinburgh & Lothians Tourist Board
Tel: 0845 2255 121
www.edinburgh.org

Visit Scottish Borders
Tel: 0845 2255 121
www.scot-borders.co.uk

Loganair
Tel: +44 (0)141 8487594
www.loganair.co.uk

Flybe
Tel: 0871 200 2000
www.flybe.com

or see **pages 157-160** for details of local historic houses, castles and gardens to visit during your stay.

For additional places to stay in the Scotland, turn to **pages 151-155** where a listing of our Recommended Hotels & Spas Guide can be found.

CRAIGELLACHIE HOTEL OF SPEYSIDE

CRAIGELLACHIE, ABERLOUR, BANFFSHIRE AB38 9SR
Tel: 01340 881204 **International:** +44 (0)1340 881204
Web: www.condenastjohansens.com/craigellachie **E-mail:** generalmanager.craigellachie@ohiml.com

Our inspector loved: The delightful recently refurbished dining room, which complements the fine award-winning menus.

Price Guide:
single £80–£120
double/twin £95–£135
four poster £125–£165

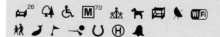

You can be sure of a warm Highland welcome at Craigellachie, a grand country hotel within spectacular surroundings. Located where the Fiddich and Spey Rivers meet at Aberlour, this an ideal spot for angling enthusiasts to land some of the world's best wild salmon due to its fast flowing current. Uninterrupted views over this breathtaking countryside are simply awe-inspiring, and for those of you in search of active pursuits, there are many to choose from. At the end of the day, there will be a inviting lounge complete with roaring log fire waiting for you or in the bar an impressive stock of over 700 whiskies can be discussed with the hotels own specialist. Fine Scottish cuisine with an emphasis on seasonal and local produce is served in the Ben Aigan Restaurant.

Awards/Recognition: 1 AA Rosettes 2011-2012

Location: Just off the A95; A9, 38 miles; Inverness Airport, 43 miles; Elgin Train Station, 10 miles

Attractions: Whiskey Trail; Fishing on River Spey; Beaches at Lossiemouth

AIRDS HOTEL

PORT APPIN, APPIN, ARGYLL PA38 4DF
Tel: 01631 730236 **International:** +44 (0)1631 730236
Web: www.condenastjohansens.com/airdshotel **E-mail:** airds@airds-hotel.com

Our inspector loved: The elegant and luxurious fusion of the old and the new, which works extremely well.

Price Guide: (including dinner)
double/twin from £260
superior from £317
suite from £342

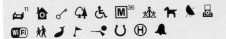

Awards/Recognition: Relais & Châteaux; 3 AA Rosettes 2011-2012; Eat Scotland Gold Award

Location: Oban, 20 miles; Fort William, 27 miles; Glasgow Airport, 135-min drive; Edinburgh Airport, 165-min drive

Attractions: Ben Nevis and gondola; Oban Whisky Distillery; Glencoe; Arduaine Gardens

Capturing the essence of the romantic retreat, Airds Hotel is a family-run luxury hotel and gourmet restaurant. Once an 18th-century ferry inn, its atmosphere is relaxed and elegant with intimate yet attentive service and its setting on the west coast of Scotland makes the most of the undulating coastline that surrounds the Appin Peninsula. The 8 bedrooms and 3 suites are warm and inviting, and vary in style from "country house" to more contemporary. Crisp Frette linens, complimentary newspapers and Bulgari toiletries add thoughtful touches, while Vi Spring beds guarantee you a good night's sleep. Some rooms feature spectacular views across Loch Linnhe and the Morvern Mountains. Reputed to be one of the best in Scotland, the inspiring restaurant led by Fellow Master Chef of Great Britain Robert MacPherson, serves an abundance of fresh ingredients from locally sourced fish and seafood to roast fillet of Scotch beef.

STONEFIELD CASTLE

TARBERT, LOCH FYNE, ARGYLL PA29 6YJ
Tel: 01880 820836 **International:** +44 (0)1880 820836
Web: www.condenastjohansens.com/stonefield **E-mail:** generalmanager.stonefieldcastle@ohiml.com

Our inspector loved: The view overlooking the sea from the dining area is quite stunning.

Price Guide: (including dinner)
single from £100
double from £120
suite from £225

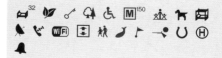

Awards/Recognition: 1 AA Rosette 2011-2012

Location: Glasgow Airport, 2-hour drive; Lochgilphead, 11 miles; Oban, 45 miles; Campbeltown, 45 miles

Attractions: Inveraray Castle and Jail; Islands of Islay, Arran and Gigha and their distilleries; Crarae Gardens

Discover the stunning 4 star Baronial Stonefield Castle near the pretty village of Tarbert on the Mull of Kintyre. Overlooking the beautiful Loch Fyne, this classic example of an elegant Victorian house stands within 60 acres of woodlands rich in azaleas and rhododrendons. The scenery in the area is quite breathtaking. Vast fireplaces, richly decorated ceilings and beautiful wood panelling have been carefully restored and now provide a stunning setting that is complemented by a warm and welcoming atmosphere that greets each guest. The dining room has some simply staggering views that look right out to sea and is the ideal setting to enjoy some of the fantastic selection of locally sourced produce that is found within the estate.

GREYWALLS AND CHEZ ROUX

MUIRFIELD, GULLANE, EAST LOTHIAN EH31 2EG
Tel: 01620 842 144 **International:** +44 (0)1620 842 144
Web: www.condenastjohansens.com/greywalls **E-mail:** enquiries@greywalls.co.uk

Our inspector loved: Enjoying lunch in a secluded area of the breathtakingly beautiful gardens.

Price Guide:
single £80-£300
double £230-£320
colonel's house from £1235

Location: Edinburgh City, 30-min drive; A1, 15 mile; Edinburgh Airport, 45-min drive

Attractions: Muirfield Golf Course; Beaches; Edinburgh Castle; Tantallon Castle; Glenkinchie Distillery

You'll find the elegance and charm of this impressive Edwardian hotel quite captivating. A relaxed, tranquil retreat set in 6 acres of walled gardens on the very edge of the historic Muirfield championship golf course, Greywalls has hosted the British Open no less than 15 times. Golf enthusiasts will never want to leave this green paradise, where 10 more challenging courses are located within 5 miles of the hotel. Homely and gracefully stylish filled with wonderful fabrics and fine antique furniture, Greywalls' guest rooms are peaceful havens. And an additional 4 bedrooms are located in a nearby self-catering Colonel's House sleeping up to 8 - ideal for a family holiday or golfing group. Expect warm Scottish hospitality, superb cuisine and spectacular links views, particularly over the 10th tee from the main dining room and of the 18th green from the manicured lawn. Managed by Inverlochy Castle Management International.

INVERLOCHY CASTLE

TORLUNDY, FORT WILLIAM PH33 6SN
Tel: 01397 702177 **International:** +44 (0)1397 702177
Web: www.condenastjohansens.com/inverlochy **E-mail:** info@inverlochy.co.uk

Our inspector loved: *The attention to detail in this luxurious castle.*

Price Guide:
single £265-£375
double £320-£440
superior £440-£550
suite £480-£695

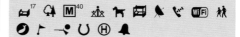

Queen Victoria's words from 1873, "I never saw a lovelier or more romantic spot," describe Inverlochy perfectly, and the first Lord Abinger who built the castle in 1863 certainly knew how to pick a gorgeous location in the foothills of Ben Nevis. Today the castle makes a splendid hotel managed by Jane Watson and first impressions of the massive reception room featuring Venetian crystal chandeliers, a Michaelangelo-style ceiling and a handsome staircase leading to 3 elaborately decorated dining rooms, carry a real 'wow' factor. Bedrooms are spacious, individually furnished and offer every comfort. Michelin-starred chef Philip Carnegie, creates modern British cuisine using local game, hand picked wild mushrooms and scallops from the Isle of Skye. Various outdoor activities await you and stunning historical landscapes are nearby. Managed by Inverlochy Castle Management International.

Awards/Recognition: Condé Nast Johansens Most Excellent Hotel Award 2008; 1 Star Michelin 2011; 3 AA Rosettes 2011-2012; Relais & Châteaux

Location: On A82; Fort William Railway Station, 4 miles; Inverness Airport, 69 miles; Glasgow Airport, 105 miles

Attractions: Ben Nevis; Glencoe; Glenfinnan; Loch Ness; The Jacobite Steam Train - aka Hogwarts Express for all Harry Potter fans

ROCPOOL RESERVE AND CHEZ ROUX

CULDUTHEL ROAD, INVERNESS, IV2 4AG
Tel: 01463 240089 **International:** +44 (0)1463 240089
Web: www.condenastjohansens.com/rocpool **E-mail:** info@rocpool.com

Our inspector loved: *The excellence of this chic, boutique hotel and classic French dishes.*

Price Guide:
hip (single) £150-£175
hip £185-£210
chic £215-£260
decadent £265-£315
extra decadent £320-£395

Awards/Recognition: Condé Nast Johansens Most Excellent City Hotel 2011; Scottish Restaurant Awards Best Newcomer Restaurant 2010

Location: City Centre, 5-min walk; Inverness Airport, 10 miles

Attractions: Castle Stuart Golf Course; Loch Ness & Caledonian Canal; Culloden Battlefield

Expect to be bowled over by Rocpool Reserve, a boutique hotel overlooking Inverness's riverside. Elegant and contemporary design harmoniously combines with classical elements, and wonderful staff offer first-class service with phenomenal attention to detail. The décor follows a colour scheme of red, black and white, and bedrooms are fitted with plasma TVs, DVD players and iPod docking stations. Enjoy the luxurious comfort of Egyptian linens, king-size beds, and Italian ceramics in bathrooms; 2 rooms even have a hot tub on the terrace! Relax during cocktail hour amidst the bar's black leather seats and sparkling chandeliers before dining in Chez Roux. This exceptional restaurant overlooks the river and serves local Scottish produce blended with classic French country cuisine, all masterminded by multi award-winning Chef Albert Henri Roux OBE. Definitely the place to stay in Europe's fastest growing city! Managed by Inverlochy Castle Management International.

Inver Lodge Hotel and Chez Roux

LOCHINVER, SUTHERLAND IV27 4LU

Tel: 01571 844496 **International:** +44 (0)1571 844496
Web: www.condenastjohansens.com/inverlodge **E-mail:** stay@inverlodge.com

Our inspector loved: The sparkling welcome in both hospitality and housekeeping.

Price Guide:
single £115–£150
double £215–£265
suite £320-£480

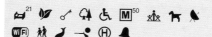

Location: Inverness Airport and Station, 2-hour drive; Lairg Railway Station, 1-hour drive

Attractions: Wild Unspoilt Scenery; Fishing on Lochs and Rivers; Bird-watching

Prepare to be stunned by Inver Lodge, a charming hotel and a haven of peace and tranquillity for those seeking a family break or romantic weekend enveloped by nature. From a hilltop perch, Inver Lodge looks down onto the quiet fishing village of Lochinver and across the waters of the loch to the distant Western Isles. Moorland reaches to the hotel doorway, red deer graze outside the windows, Atlantic seals pop up in the harbour and golden eagles soar over the mountains! End the perfect day by enjoying a relaxing chat and drink in the oh-so welcoming foyer lounge before sampling the delights of the exceptional Chez Roux restaurant where famed Chef Albert Roux OBE serves "hearty country cooking." Then retire to your delightfully comfortable bedroom and admire the spectacular sea view. Managed by Inverlochy Castle Management International.

Like you, we're
recommended
by Condé Nast Johansens

As the preferred insurance partner of Condé Nast Johansens, JLT is best placed to make a first class difference to your insurance needs.

JLT has a specialist team with over 20 years experience in the global hotel industry. Our clients include some of the worlds most luxurious hotels.

The difference comes from our understanding of the way we present your risks to the insurance market and work with underwriters to maximise the best terms for you. Through our enthusiasm, attention to detail and commitment, we can build you a tailor-made solution set around your individual requirements at a competitive price.

To learn more about JLT contact
Sanjay Patel • +44 (0)20 7528 4641 • sanjay_patel@jltgroup.com

JLT

Insurance Broking • Innovation
Risk Identification and Management • Disaster Recovery

Wales

Holyhead

A55

A55

A5

Llandudno

144

A470

A55

Caernarfon

A487

A5

145

A470

Wrexham

A483

A534

Snowdonia National Park

A494

A5

A470

A494

Dolgellau

146

148

A458

A487

A470

A483

A470

A44

Aberystwyth

A470

A470

A483

A487

A44

A44

A487

A483

149

A470

Fishguard

A40

A483

A470

A438

A40

Brecon

A479

A40

A487

A40

Carmarthen

A40

A470

A40

Pembroke

A40

147

A477

A48

A483

Brecon Beacons National Park

Abergavenny

A40

Swansea

M4

A465

A449

M4

M4

A470

Cardiff

Cardiff

ENGLAND

Wales

For further information on Wales, please contact:

Wales Tourist Board
Tel: 0845 010 3300
www.visitwales.com

North Wales Tourism
Tel: 0845 450 5885
www.nwt.co.uk

Mid Wales Tourism
E-mail: info@midwalestourism.co.uk
www.visitmidwales.co.uk

South West Wales Tourism Partnership
Tel: +44 (0)1558 669091
www.swwtp.co.uk

Cadw: Welsh Historic Monuments
Tel: +44 (0)1443 33 6000
E-mail: cadw@wales.gsi.gov.uk
www.cadw.wales.gov.uk

Millennium Stadium
Tel: 08442 777 888
www.millenniumstadium.com

or see **pages 157-160** for details of local historic houses, castles and gardens to visit during your stay.

For additional places to stay in the Wales, turn to **pages 151-155** where a listing of our Recommended Hotels & Spas Guide can be found.

Penmaenuchaf Hall, Gwtnedd, Wales – p146

St Tudno Hotel & Restaurant

NORTH PROMENADE, LLANDUDNO, NORTH WALES LL30 2LP
Tel: 01492 874411 **International:** +44 (0)1492 874411
Web: www.condenastjohansens.com/sttudno **E-mail:** sttudnohotel@btinternet.com

Our inspector loved: The warm welcome and friendly staff at this charming sea front hotel.

Price Guide:
single from £75
double/twin £95–£220
suite from £250

Awards/Recognition: 2 AA Rosettes 2011-2012

Location: On the A470; A55, 4 miles; Chester, 45 miles; Manchester Airport, 65 miles

Attractions: Theatre at Llandudno; Bodnant Gardens; Dry Ski Slope and Tobaggan run on the Great Orme; Conwy & Caernarfon Castles

Undoubtedly one of the most delightful small hotels in Wales and indeed to be found on the coast of Britain, St Tudno (now in its 40th year) offers a very special experience. A former winner of the Johansen's Hotel of the Year Award for Excellence, the elegantly and lovingly refurbished hotel provides a particularly warm welcome from Martin Bland and his staff. The individually designed bedrooms have many thoughtful extras and the Terrace Restaurant is regarded as one of Wales' leading places to eat. A little oasis at this town house is the indoor heated swimming pool and secret garden. This 3 AA Red Star Hotel has won a host of awards: Best Seaside Resort Hotel in Great Britain (Good Hotel Guide), Welsh Hotel of the Year, 2 major wine awards and even an accolade for having the Best Hotel Loos in Britain. Ideally situated for visits to Snowdonia National Park, world famous Bodnant Gardens, Anglesey and glorious walks on the Great Orme.

RUTHIN CASTLE HOTEL

RUTHIN, DENBIGHSHIRE LL15 2NU

Tel: 01824 702664 **International:** +44 (0)1824 702664

Web: www.condenastjohansens.com/ruthincastle **E-mail:** reception@ruthincastle.co.uk

Our inspector loved: *The Jesters feast at this historic Welsh castle.*

Price Guide:
single from £80
double £99-180
suite £200-330

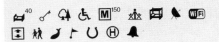

Awards/Recognition: 2 AA Rosettes 2011-2012

Location: A525, 0.5 miles; A55, 8 miles; Chester, 22 miles; Conwy, 23 miles

Attractions: Snowdonia National Park; Historic City of Chester; North Wales Coast; Clwyd Hills

Set amidst 30 acres of breathtaking woods and parkland, this romantic hotel is steeped in history with a rich royal heritage counting King Edward I, Henry VIII and Elizabeth I amongst its owners. The castle, which dates back prior to 1277 and the legend of King Arthur, is now a welcoming hotel with 40 individually styled bedrooms to suit every budget; for the ultimate stay be sure to choose one of the 4 unusually themed and extravagantly furnished Royal Salons. Innovative pan-European cooking, based on only the freshest of local ingredients, is available at Bertie's, which has received numerous prestigious accolades. And activities on-site and nearby include Jesters feast held in the oldest standing part of the Castle, picturesque walks through the gardens, which feature an original walled dry moat, exploring the castle ruins, white-water rafting and discovering scenic coast of Northern Wales and Snowdonia.

PENMAENUCHAF HALL

PENMAENPOOL, DOLGELLAU, GWYNEDD LL40 1YB
Tel: 01341 422129 **International:** +44 (0)1341 422129
Web: www.condenastjohansens.com/penmaenuchafhall **E-mail:** relax@penhall.co.uk

Our inspector loved: The owners care and attention to their guests, an award winning hotel with beautiful gardens.

Price Guide:
single £100–£150
double/twin £160–£250

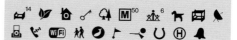

From the moment you've climbed the long tree-lined driveway, you'll relax and enjoy this glorious setting. Nestled near Dolgellau in the Snowdownia National Park, this award-winning hotel offers stunning views across the Mawddach Estuary to distant wooded mountain slopes. The Hall is a Victorian build maintaining its original oak and mahogany panelling, stained glass windows, slate floors and log fires in winter. The 21-acre grounds blend lawns, both a water and lavender garden and woodland. Guest's can enjoy bedrooms showcasing fabulous balconies and the Garden Room restaurant, where food lovers can dine on imaginative, seasonal dishes. Spend your break fishing along 10 miles of the Mawddach River or the 'llyn Penmaenuchaf' within the hotel's grounds, mountain biking, visiting sandy beaches or playing championship golf courses. Penmaenuchaf Hall won the accolade AA Hotel of the Year Wales 2011 and the Visit Wales Gold Award 2010-2011.

Awards/Recognition: Condé Nast Johansens Most Excellent Country House Hotel 2011; Condé Nast Johansens and Champagne Taittinger Wine List Awards, Special Commendation - Education of the Customer 2011; 1 AA Rosettes 2010-2011

Location: A493, 0.5 mile; A470, 1.5 miles; Shrewsbury, 60 miles; Chester, 60 miles

Attractions: Snowdonia National Park; Narrow Guage Railways; Bodnant Garden; Portmeirion

THE GROVE HOTEL

MOLLESTON, NARBERTH, PEMBROKESHIRE SA67 8BX
Tel: 01834 860 915 **International:** +44 (0)1834 860 915
Web: www.condenastjohansens.com/grovenarberth **E-mail:** info@thegrove-narberth.co.uk

Our inspector loved: *The traditional bedrooms with a contemporary twist and conservatory-style breakfast room.*

Price Guide:
single £140-£280
double £150-£290

Awards/Recognition: 2 AA Rosettes 2011-2012

Location: A4115, 1.3 miles; A478, 2 miles; A40, 10 miles; Tenby, 10 miles

Attractions: Pembrokeshire Coastal National Park and its beaches; St Davids and its Cathedral; Skomer Island; National Botanical Gardens of Wales

Nestled amidst the rolling hills of beautiful Pembrokeshire and with breathtaking views of the Preseli Mountains, this charming 18th-century country house is impressive both inside and out. One of the most intimate and unique luxury hotels in Wales, and steeped in history, The Grove Hotel offers 9 individually designed guest rooms and 3 characterful suites surrounded by 26 acres of scenic grounds. Each bedroom and suite is filled with luxurious Zoffany and Melin Tregwynt furnishings and displays beautiful local and international artwork. Guests in need of serious pampering will love the deep cast-iron baths, underfloor heating and wonderful in-room aromatherapy massages. The restaurant presents a truly sumptuous dining experience, serving modern British food creatively prepared from seasonal and locally sourced ingredients.

Lake Vyrnwy Hotel & Spa

LAKE VYRNWY, LLANWDDYN, POWYS SY10 0LY
Tel: 01691 870 692 **International:** +44 (0)1691 870 692
Web: www.condenastjohansens.com/lakevyrnwy **E-mail:** info@lakevyrnwyhotel.co.uk

Our inspector loved: *Enjoying the spectacular views from the balcony of the new look refurbished Tavern.*

Price Guide:
single £100–£200
double/twin £125–£178
premier double £198–£225

Awards/Recognition: 1 AA Rosette 2011-2012

Location: A490, 8 miles; A495, 12 miles; Shrewsbury, 35 miles; Chester, 50 miles

Attractions: Powis Castle; Snowdonia National Park; Portmeirion; Centre for Alternative Technology; Little Railways of Wales

The location of Lake Vyrnwy Hotel & Spa is just magical, overlooking the stunning lake and surrounded by wild moorland, forest and the rugged Berwyn Mountains. A picturesque getaway enveloped by walking trails and opportunities for clay shooting, fishing, water sports and cycling, this wonderful setting can be admired through the windows of the warm and inviting drawing room from sumptuous sofas and balconies located off most bedrooms. As the sun goes down the Tower Bar's balcony is the perfect place to savour a glass of wine before enjoying dinner in the restaurant where the menus reflect a genuine enthusiasm for food and utilise as much local produce as possible. The newly styled contemporary Tavern Bar is ideal for more informal dining. Why not pamper yourself in the luxury spa and thermal suite, with its extensive range of therapies and array of facilities that include an Arabian rasul mud therapy chamber and Monsoon shower.

LAKE COUNTRY HOUSE & SPA

LLANGAMMARCH WELLS, POWYS LD4 4BS
Tel: 01591 620202 **International:** +44 (0)1591 620202
Web: www.condenastjohansens.com/lakecountryhouse **E-mail:** info@lakecountryhouse.co.uk

Our inspector loved: *This hotel and spa is the perfect place for relaxation and outdoor pursuits.*

Price Guide:
single from £145
superior from £195
suite from £240

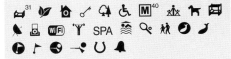

Awards/Recognition: Condé Nast Johansens Most Excellent Spa 2009; 2 AA Rosettes 2011-2012

Location: A 485, 3 miles; A 470, 8 miles; Hay on Wye, 21 miles; Cardiff Airport, 52 miles

Attractions: Brecon Beacons National Park; Cambrian Mountains & Elan Valley; Aberglasney House and Gardens; Raglan Castle

Trouts leaping up from a serene lake, otters in the river, carpets of wild flowers bobbing in the breeze and badgers ambling by the woods nearby are all sights to be savoured at Lake Country House with luxury spa, surrounded by 50 acres of unspoilt land. This hidden gem is a haven for wildlife enthusiasts with over 100 bird-nesting boxes within the grounds and ample opportunities for fishing and horse riding. Feast on traditional Welsh teas by a roaring log fire in one of the decadent lounges during winter or beneath the chestnut tree during summer. Enjoy fresh produce and herbs from the garden in the restaurant and sample some of the superb wines from the list of over 300 bins. To complete your stay, why not visit the Condé Nast Johansens award-winning lakeside spa; an inspired setting to unwind and totally relax.

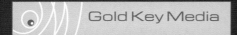

Small Hotels, Inns & Restaurants - Great Britain & Ireland

Properties listed below can be found in our Recommended Small Hotels, Inns & Restaurants – Great Britain & Ireland 2012 Guide

CHANNEL ISLANDS - GUERNSEY (SARK)

La Sablonnerie

Little Sark, Sark, Guernsey GY9 0SD

Tel: 01481 832061
www.condenastjohansens.com/lasablonnerie

CUMBRIA - WINDERMERE

Cedar Manor Hotel

Ambleside Road, Windermere, Cumbria LA23 1AX

Tel: 015394 43192
www.condenastjohansens.com/cedarmanor

CHANNEL ISLANDS - JERSEY (ROZEL BAY)

Château La Chaire

Rozel Bay, Jersey JE3 6AJ

Tel: 01534 863354
www.condenastjohansens.com/chateaulachaire

CUMBRIA - WINDERMERE

The Windermere Suites

New Road, Windermere, Cumbria LA23 2LA

Tel: 015394 44739
www.condenastjohansens.com/windermeresuites

BEDFORDSHIRE - COLMWORTH (BEDFORD)

Cornfields Restaurant & Hotel

Wilden Road, Colmworth, Bedfordshire MK44 2NJ

Tel: 01234 378990
www.condenastjohansens.com/cornfields

CUMBRIA - WINDERMERE (BOWNESS)

Fayrer Garden House Hotel

Lyth Valley Road, Bowness-on-Windermere, Cumbria LA23 3JP

Tel: 015394 88195
www.condenastjohansens.com/fayrergarden

BEDFORDSHIRE - WOBURN (FLITWICK)

Flitwick Manor

Church Road, Flitwick, Bedfordshire MK45 1AE

Tel: 01525 712242
www.condenastjohansens.com/flitwickmanor

CUMBRIA - WINDERMERE (TROUTBECK)

Broadoaks Country House

Bridge Lane, Troutbeck, Windermere, Cumbria LA23 1LA

Tel: 01539 445566
www.condenastjohansens.com/broadoaks

CORNWALL - BUDE

Elements Hotel and Restaurant

Marine Drive, Widemouth Bay, Bude, Cornwall EX23 0LZ

Tel: 01288 352386
www.condenastjohansens.com/elements

DERBYSHIRE - BAKEWELL (DARLEY DALE)

Holmefield Country Guest House

Dale Road North, Darley Dale, Near Bakewell, Matlock, Derbyshire DE4 2HY

Tel: 01629 735347
www.condenastjohansens.com/holmefield

CORNWALL - LIZARD

Atlantic House

Pentreath Lane, Lizard, Cornwall TR12 7NY

Tel: 01326 290399
www.condenastjohansens.com/atlantichselizard

DEVON - BABBACOMBE

The Cary Arms

Babbacombe Beach, South Devon TQ1 3LX

Tel: 01803 327110
www.condenastjohansens.com/caryarms

CORNWALL - ST IVES

The Garrack Hotel & Restaurant

Burthallan Lane, St Ives, Cornwall TR26 3AA

Tel: 01736 796199
www.condenastjohansens.com/garrack

DEVON - ILFRACOMBE

The Hampton's Hotel

Excelsior Villas, Torrs Park, Ilfracombe, Devon EX34 8AZ

Tel: 01271 864246
www.condenastjohansens.com/hamptonshotel

CUMBRIA - WINDERMERE

Applegarth Villa

College Road, Windermere, Cumbria LA23 1BU

Tel: 015394 43206
www.condenastjohansens.com/applegarth

DEVON - MARTINHOE (EXMOOR NATIONAL PARK)

The Old Rectory Hotel

Martinhoe, Exmoor National Park, Devon EX31 4QT

Tel: 01598 763368
www.condenastjohansens.com/oldrectoryexmoor

Small Hotels, Inns & Restaurants - Great Britain & Ireland

Properties listed below can be found in our Recommended Small Hotels, Inns & Restaurants – Great Britain & Ireland 2012 Guide

DEVON - STAVERTON (NEAR TOTNES)

Kingston House

Staverton, Near Totnes, Devon TQ9 6AR

Tel: 01803 762 235
www.condenastjohansens.com/kingstonhouse

HAMPSHIRE - BROCKENHURST

The Pig Hotel

Beaulieu Road, Brockenhurst, New Forest, Hampshire SO42 7QL

Tel: 01590 622354
www.condenastjohansens.com/thepig

DEVON - TAVISTOCK (GULWORTHY)

The Horn of Plenty Hotel & Restaurant

Gulworthy, Tavistock, Devon PL19 8JD

Tel: 01822 832528
www.condenastjohansens.com/thehornofplenty

HAMPSHIRE - LYMINGTON (HORDLE)

The Mill At Gordleton

Silver Street, Hordle, Nr Lymington, New Forest, Hampshire SO41 6DJ

Tel: 01590 682219
www.condenastjohansens.com/themillatgordleton

DORSET - SHERBORNE (OBORNE)

The Grange at Oborne

Oborne, Near Sherborne, Dorset DT9 4LA

Tel: 01935 813463
www.condenastjohansens.com/grangesherborne

HEREFORDSHIRE - HEREFORD

Aylestone Court

Aylestone Hill, Hereford, Herefordshire HR1 1HS

Tel: 01432 341891
www.condenastjohansens.com/aylestonecourt

ESSEX - SOUTHEND-ON-SEA

Pier View

5 Royal Terrace, Southend-on-Sea, Essex SS1 1DY

Tel: 01702 437 900
www.condenastjohansens.com/pierview

HEREFORDSHIRE - ROSS-ON-WYE

Wilton Court

Wilton, Ross-on-Wye, Herefordshire HR9 6AQ

Tel: 01989 562569
www.condenastjohansens.com/wiltoncourthotel

GLOUCESTERSHIRE - BIBURY (COTSWOLDS)

The Swan Hotel

Bibury, Gloucestershire GL7 5NW

Tel: 01285 740695
www.condenastjohansens.com/swanhotelbibury

ISLE OF WIGHT - SEAVIEW

The Priory Bay Hotel

Priory Drive, Seaview, Isle of Wight PO34 5BU

Tel: 01983 613146
www.condenastjohansens.com/priorybayiow

GLOUCESTERSHIRE - MORETON-IN-MARSH

The White Hart Royal Hotel

High Street, Moreton-in-Marsh, Gloucestershire GL56 0BA

Tel: 01608 650731
www.condenastjohansens.com/whitehartroyal

ISLE OF WIGHT - SHANKLIN

Rylstone Manor

Rylstone Gardens, Shanklin, Isle of Wight PO37 6RG

Tel: 01983 862806
www.condenastjohansens.com/rylstonemanor

GLOUCESTERSHIRE - MORETON-IN-MARSH (BLOCKLEY)

Lower Brook House

Blockley, Nr Moreton-in-Marsh, Gloucestershire GL56 9DS

Tel: 01386 700286
www.condenastjohansens.com/lowerbrookhouse

KENT - DOVER (WEST CLIFFE)

Wallett's Court Hotel & Spa

West Cliffe, St Margaret's-at-Cliffe, Dover, Kent CT15 6EW

Tel: 01304 852424
www.condenastjohansens.com/wallettscourt

GLOUCESTERSHIRE - NEWENT

Three Choirs Vineyards Estate

Newent, Gloucestershire GL18 1LS

Tel: 01531 890223
www.condenastjohansens.com/threechoirs

KENT - TENTERDEN (NEAR ASHFORD)

Little Silver Country Hotel

Ashford Road, St Michaels, Tenterden, Kent TN30 6SP

Tel: 01233 850321
www.condenastjohansens.com/littlesilver

Small Hotels, Inns & Restaurants - Great Britain & Ireland

Properties listed below can be found in our Recommended Small Hotels, Inns & Restaurants – Great Britain & Ireland 2012 Guide

LANCASHIRE - PRESTON (LONGRIDGE)

Ferrari's Restaurant & Hotel

Thornley, Longridge, Preston, Lancashire PR3 2TB

Tel: 01772 783148

www.condenastjohansens.com/ferraris

OXFORDSHIRE - OXFORD (MURCOTT)

The Nut Tree Pub

Murcott, Kidlington, Oxfordshire OX5 2RE

Tel: 01865 331253

www.condenastjohansens.com/nuttreeinn

NORFOLK - NORWICH (THORPE ST ANDREW)

The Old Rectory

103 Yarmouth Road, Norwich, Norfolk NR7 0HF

Tel: 01603 700772

www.condenastjohansens.com/oldrectorynorwich

SHROPSHIRE - OSWESTRY

Pen-Y-Dyffryn Country Hotel

Rhydycroesau, Near Oswestry, Shropshire SY10 7JD

Tel: 01691 653700

www.condenastjohansens.com/penydyffryn

NORTHUMBERLAND - BAMBURGH

Waren House Hotel

Waren Mill, Bamburgh, Northumberland NE70 7EE

Tel: 01668 214581

www.condenastjohansens.com/warenhouse

SHROPSHIRE - SHREWSBURY (WEM)

Soulton Hall

Near Wem, Shropshire SY4 5RS

Tel: 01939 232786

www.condenastjohansens.com/soultonhall

NOTTINGHAMSHIRE - ARNOLD (NEAR NOTTINGHAM)

Cockliffe Country House Hotel

Burntstump Country Park, Burntstump Hill, Arnold, Nottinghamshire NG5 8PQ

Tel: 0115 968 0179

www.condenastjohansens.com/cockliffe

SOMERSET - AXBRIDGE (NEAR CHEDDAR)

Compton House

Townsend, Axbridge, Somerset BS26 2AJ

Tel: 01934 733944

www.condenastjohansens.com/comptonhouse

NOTTINGHAMSHIRE - NOTTINGHAM

Greenwood Lodge

5 Third Avenue, Sherwood Rise, Nottingham NG7 6JH

Tel: 0115 962 1206

www.condenastjohansens.com/greenwoodlodge

SOMERSET - MINEHEAD

Binham Grange

Old Cleeve, Near Minehead, Somerset TA24 6HX

Tel: 01984 640056

www.condenastjohansens.com/binhamgrange

OXFORDSHIRE - BURFORD (COTSWOLDS)

Burford House

99 High Street, Burford, Oxfordshire OX18 4QA

Tel: 01993 823151

www.condenastjohansens.com/burfordhouse

SOMERSET - SHEPTON MALLET

Bowlish House

Wells Road, Bowlish, Shepton Mallet, Somerset BA4 5JD

Tel: 01749 342022

www.condenastjohansens.com/bowlishhouse

OXFORDSHIRE - BURFORD (COTSWOLDS)

The Lamb Inn

Sheep Street, Burford, Oxfordshire OX18 4LR

Tel: 01993 823155

www.condenastjohansens.com/lambinnburford

SOMERSET - WELLS

Beryl

Wells, Somerset BA5 3JP

Tel: 01749 678738

www.condenastjohansens.com/beryl

OXFORDSHIRE - OXFORD (MINSTER LOVELL)

Old Swan & Minster Mill

Minster Lovell, Near Burford, Oxfordshire OX29 0RN

Tel: 01993 774441

www.condenastjohansens.com/milloldswan

STAFFORDSHIRE - MODDERSHALL (NEAR STONE)

Moddershall Oaks Spa Restaurant Suites

Moddershall, Stone, Staffordshire ST15 8TG

Tel: 01782 399000

www.condenastjohansens.com/moddershalloaks

Small Hotels, Inns & Restaurants - Great Britain & Ireland

Properties listed below can be found in our Recommended Small Hotels, Inns & Restaurants – Great Britain & Ireland 2012 Guide

SUFFOLK - BURY ST. EDMUNDS

Clarice House

Horringer Court, Horringer Road, Bury St Edmunds, Suffolk IP29 5PH

Tel: 01284 705550
www.condenastjohansens.com/clarice

WORCESTERSHIRE - UPTON-UPON-SEVERN (NEAR MALVERN)

The White Lion Hotel

High Street, Upton-upon-Severn, Near Malvern, Worcestershire WR8 0HJ

Tel: 01684 592551
www.condenastjohansens.com/whitelionupton

SUFFOLK - EYE (BROME)

The Cornwallis Country Hotel & Restaurant

Brome, Eye, Suffolk IP23 8AJ

Tel: 01379 870326
www.condenastjohansens.com/cornwallis

NORTH YORKSHIRE - AUSTWICK (YORKSHIRE DALES)

The Traddock

Austwick, North Yorkshire LA2 8BY

Tel: 015242 51224
www.condenastjohansens.com/austwick

SUFFOLK - MILDENHALL (NEAR NEWMARKET)

The Olde Bull Inn

Barton Mills, Bury St Edmunds, Suffolk IP28 6AA

Tel: 01638 711001
www.condenastjohansens.com/oldebullinn

NORTH YORKSHIRE - WHITBY

Dunsley Hall

Dunsley, Whitby, North Yorkshire YO21 3TL

Tel: 01947 893437
www.condenastjohansens.com/dunsleyhall

SUFFOLK - SAXMUNDHAM (YOXFORD)

Satis House Hotel & Restaurant

Main Road, Yoxford, Saxmundham, Suffolk IP17 3EX

Tel: 01728 668418
www.condenastjohansens.com/satishouse

WEST YORKSHIRE - MARSDEN

Hey Green Country House Hotel

Waters Road, Marsden, West Yorkshire HD7 6NG

Tel: 01484 848000
www.condenastjohansens.com/heygreen

SURREY - CHIDDINGFOLD

The Crown Inn

The Green, Petworth Road, Chiddingfold, Surrey GU8 4TX

Tel: 01428 682255
www.condenastjohansens.com/crownchiddingfold

DUBLIN - DUBLIN

The Cliff Town House

22 St Stephen's Green, Dublin

Tel: 00 353 1 638 3939
www.condenastjohansens.com/clifftownhouse

SURREY - CHIDDINGFOLD

The Swan Inn

Petworth Road, Chiddingfold, Surrey GU8 4TY

Tel: 01428 684688
www.condenastjohansens.com/swansurrey

MONAGHAN - GLASLOUGH

Castle Leslie

Castle Leslie Estate, Glaslough, County Monaghan

Tel: 00 353 47 88100
www.condenastjohansens.com/castleleslie

WILTSHIRE - CASTLE COMBE

The Castle Inn

Castle Combe, Wiltshire SN14 7HN

Tel: 01249 783030
www.condenastjohansens.com/castleinn

ARGYLL & BUTE - DUNOON AND OBAN

The Majestic Line - Argyll Coast Cruises

3 Melville Crescent, Edinburgh EH3 7HW

Tel: 0131 623 5012
www.condenastjohansens.com/themajesticline

WORCESTERSHIRE - IPSLEY (NEAR REDDITCH)

The Old Rectory

Ipsley Lane, Ipsley, Near Redditch, Worcestershire B98 0AP

Tel: 01527 523000
www.condenastjohansens.com/oldrecipsley

ARGYLL & BUTE - OBAN

The Manor House Hotel

Gallanach Road, Oban, Argyll & Bute PA34 4LS

Tel: 01631 562087
www.condenastjohansens.com/manorhouseoban

Small Hotels, Inns & Restaurants - Great Britain & Ireland

Properties listed below can be found in our Recommended Small Hotels, Inns & Restaurants – Great Britain & Ireland 2012 Guide

DUMFRIES & GALLOWAY - AUCHENCAIRN (CASTLE DOUGLAS)

Balcary Bay Hotel

Auchencairn, Castle Douglas, Dumfries & Galloway DG7 1QZ

Tel: 01556 640217/640311
www.condenastjohansens.com/balcarybay

DUMFRIES & GALLOWAY - KIRKPATRICK DURHAM (NEAR DUMFRIES)

Craigadam

Kirkpatrick Durham, Kirkcudbrightshire DG7 3HU

Tel: 01556 650233
www.condenastjohansens.com/craigadam

DUMFRIES & GALLOWAY - STRANRAER (NEAR KIRKCOLM)

Corsewall Lighthouse Hotel

Corsewall Point, Near Kirkcolm, Stranraer, DG9 0QG

Tel: 01776 853220
www.condenastjohansens.com/lighthousehotel

HIGHLAND - INVERNESS

Loch Ness Lodge

Brachla, Loch Ness-side, Inverness IV3 8LA

Tel: 01456 459469
www.condenastjohansens.com/lochnesslodge

HIGHLAND - NAIRN

Clubhouse Hotel

45 Seabank Road, Nairn, Inverness-shire IV12 4EY

Tel: 01667 453321
www.condenastjohansens.com/clubhousenairn

HIGHLAND - NAIRN

Inveran Lodge

Seafield Street, Nairn, Inverness-shire IV12 4HG

Tel: 01667 455 666
www.condenastjohansens.com/inveranlodge

HIGHLAND - SOUTH LOCH NESS (BY INVERNESS)

The Steadings at The Grouse & Trout

Flichity by Farr, South Loch Ness, Inverness IV2 6XD

Tel: 01808 521314
www.condenastjohansens.com/steadings

CEREDIGION - CARDIGAN (GLYNARTHEN)

Penbontbren

Glynarthen, Near Cardigan, Llandysul, Ceredigion SA44 6PE

Tel: 01239 810248
www.condenastjohansens.com/penbontbren

CONWY - CONWY (SYCHNANT PASS)

Sychnant Pass Country House

Sychnant Pass Road, Conwy LL32 8BJ

Tel: 01492 596868
www.condenastjohansens.com/sychnantpass

GWYNEDD - ABERSOCH

Porth Tocyn Country House Hotel

Abersoch, Pwllheli, Gwynedd LL53 7BU

Tel: 01758 713303
www.condenastjohansens.com/porthtocyn

GWYNEDD - BARMOUTH

Bae Abermaw

Panorama Hill, Barmouth, Gwynedd LL42 1DQ

Tel: 01341 280550
www.condenastjohansens.com/baeabermaw

GWYNEDD - BARMOUTH (LLANABER)

Llwyndu Farmhouse

Llanaber, Nr Barmouth, Gwynedd LL42 1RR

Tel: 01341 280144
www.condenastjohansens.com/llwyndu

GWYNEDD - CAERNARFON

Plas Dinas Country House

Bontnewydd, Caernarfon, Gwynedd LL54 7YF

Tel: 01286 830214
www.condenastjohansens.com/plasdinas

MONMOUTHSHIRE - MONMOUTH (SKENFRITH)

The Bell At Skenfrith

Skenfrith, Monmouthshire NP7 8UH

Tel: 01600 750235
www.condenastjohansens.com/bellskenfrith

MONMOUTHSHIRE - TREDUNNOCK (NEAR USK)

Newbridge On Usk

Tredunnock, Near Usk, Monmouthshire NP15 1LY

Tel: 01633 451000
www.condenastjohansens.com/newbridgeonusk

MONMOUTHSHIRE - WHITEBROOK (MONMOUTH)

The Crown At Whitebrook

Whitebrook, Monmouthshire NP25 4TX

Tel: 01600 860254
www.condenastjohansens.com/crownatwhitebrook

L'OCCITANE
EN PROVENCE

A true story

The scents and traditions of the land of Provence lie at the heart of L'OCCITANE. It has gained its most precious secrets from this unique region, where Nature is so beautiful and flowers have long yielded their benefits.

From their harvests come natural and authentic skincare products, fragrances and toiletries, effective and deliciously tempting.

www.loccitane.com

Experience L'OCCITANE amenities in the best properties around the world. L'OCCITANE is proud to be a Condé Nast Johansens Preferred Partner.

Historic Houses, Castles & Gardens

We are pleased to feature over 170 places to visit during your stay at a Condé Nast Johansens Recommendation.
More information about these attractions, including opening times and entry fees, can be found on www.historichouses.co.uk

Channel Islands

Guernsey

Sausmarez Manor – Sausmarez Road, St Martin, Guernsey GY4 6SG. Tel: 01481 235571

England

Bath & North East Somerset

Cothay Manor and Gardens – Greenham, Wellington, Bath & North East Somerset TA21 0JR. Tel: 01823 672283
Maunsel House – North Newton, Nr Taunton, Bath & North East Somerset TA7 0BU. Tel: 01278 661076

Bedfordshire

John Bunyan Museum & Library – Bunyan Meeting Free Church, Mill Street, Bedford, Bedfordshire MK40 3EU. Tel: 01234 270303
Moggerhanger Park – Park Road, Moggerhanger, Bedfordshire MK44 3RW. Tel: 01767 641007

Berkshire

Eton College – The Visits Office, Eton High Street, Windsor, Berkshire SL4 6DW. Tel: 01753 671177

Buckinghamshire

Nether Winchendon House – Nr Aylesbury, Buckinghamshire HP18 0DY. Tel: 01844 290101
Stowe House – Stowe, Buckinghamshire MK18 5EH. Tel: 01280 818166 24 Hour Recorded enquiries line / 01280 8181229 Office hour enquiries
Waddesdon Manor – Waddesdon, Nr Aylesbury, Buckinghamshire HP18 0JH. Tel: 01296 653226

Cambridgeshire

Island Hall – Post Street, Godmanchester, Cambridgeshire PE29 2BA. Tel: 01480 459676
The Manor – Hemingford Grey, Huntingdon, Cambridgeshire PE28 9BN. Tel: 01480 463134
Oliver Cromwell's House – 29 St Mary's Street, Ely, Cambridgeshire CB7 4HF. Tel: 01353 662062

Cheshire

Dorfold Hall – Nantwich, Cheshire CW5 8LD. Tel: 01270 625245
Norton Priory Museum & Garden – Tudor Road, Manor Park, Runcorn, Cheshire WA7 1SX. Tel: 01928 569895
Rode Hall and Gardens – Scholar Green, Cheshire ST7 3QP. Tel: 01270 882961 / 873237
Tabley House Collection – Knutsford, Cheshire WA16 0HB. Tel: 01565 750 151

Cornwall

Caerhays Castle – Estate Office, Gorran, St. Austell, Cornwall PL26 6LY. Tel: 01872 501310 /501144
Mount Edgcumbe House & Country Park – Cremyll, Torpoint, Cornwall PL10 1HZ. Tel: 01752 822236
Pencarrow House and Gardens – Washway, Bodmin, Cornwall PL30 3AG. Tel: 01208 841369
Port Eliot House – Port Eliot Estate Office, St Germans, Saltash, Cornwall PL12 5ND. Tel: 01503 230211
Prideaux Place – Padstow, Cornwall PL28 8RP. Tel: 01841 532411

Cumbria

Dove Cottage & The Wordsworth Museum – The Wordsworth Trust, Dove Cottage, Grasmere, Cumbria LA22 9SH. Tel: 015394 35544
Isel Hall – Cockermouth, Cumbria CA13 0QG. Tel: 01900 826127 / 812436
Townend – Troutbeck, Windermere, Cumbria LA23 1LB. Tel: 015394 32628

Derbyshire

Hardwick Hall, Gardens, Park & Mill – The National Trust, Doe Lea, Chesterfield, Derbyshire S44 5QJ. Tel: 01246 858400
Melbourne Hall & Gardens – Melbourne, Derbyshire DE73 8EN. Tel: 01332 862502
Renishaw Hall and Gardens – Nr Sheffield, Derbyshire S21 3WB. Tel: 01246 432210

Devon

Bowringsleigh – Kingsbridge, Devon TQ7 3LL. Tel: 01548 857648 / 01548 852014
Downes – Crediton, Devon EX17 3PL. Tel: 01363 775142
Powderham Castle – Kenton, Exeter, Devon EX6 8JQ. Tel: 01626 890243

Dorset

Chiffchaffs – Chaffeymoor, Bourton, Gillingham, Dorset SP8 5BY. Tel: 01747 840841
Moignes Court – Owermoigne, Dorchester, Dorset DT2 8HY. Tel: 01305 853300
Russell-Cotes Art Gallery & Museum – Russell-Cotes Road, East Cliff, Bournemouth, Dorset BH1 3AA. Tel: 01202 451858

Durham

Raby Castle – Staindrop, Darlington, Durham DL2 3AH. Tel: 01833 660 202

Essex

Hedingham Castle – Bayley Street, Castle Hedingham, Nr Halstead, Essex CO9 3DJ. Tel: 01787 460261

Ingatestone Hall – Hall Lane, Ingatestone, Essex CM4 9NR. Tel: 01277 353010

Historic Houses, Castles & Gardens

We are pleased to feature over 170 places to visit during your stay at a Condé Nast Johansens Recommendation. More information about these attractions, including opening times and entry fees, can be found on www.historichouses.co.uk

Gloucestershire

Cheltenham Art Gallery & Museum – Clarence Street, Cheltenham, Gloucestershire GL50 3JT. Tel: 01242 237431
Frampton Court – Frampton-on-Severn, Gloucester, Gloucestershire GL2 7DY. Tel: 01452 740698
Hardwicke Court – Nr Gloucester, Gloucestershire GL2 4RS. Tel: 01452 720212
Nature In Art - Wallsworth Hall – Wallsworth Hall, Main A38, Twigworth, Gloucestershire GL2 9PA. Tel: 01452 731422
Sezincote House & Garden – Moreton-in-Marsh, Gloucestershire GL56 9AW. Tel: 01386 700444

Hampshire

Avington Park – Winchester, Hampshire SO21 1DB. Tel: 01962 779260

Beaulieu – Beaulieu Enterprises Ltd, John Montagu Bldg, Hampshire SO42 7ZN. Tel: 01590 614680
Broadlands – Romsey, Hampshire SO51 9ZD. Tel: 01794 529750/ 741
Buckler's Hard – Beaulieu, Brockenhurst, Hampshire SO42 7XB. Tel: 01590 616203
Gilbert White's House & Garden & The Oates Collection – High Street, Selborne, Nr Alton, Hampshire GU34 3JH. Tel: 01420 511275
Greywell Hill House – Greywell, Hook, Hampshire RG29 1DG. Tel: 01256 703565

Isle of Wight

Deacons Nursery (H.H) – Moor View, Godshill, Isle of Wight PO38 3HW. Tel: 01983 840750 or 522243

Kent

Belmont House – Belmont Park, Throwley, Faversham, Kent ME13 0HH. Tel: 01795 890202
Cobham Hall – Cobham, Nr Gravesend, Kent DA12 3BL. Tel: 01474 823371
The Grange – Ramsgate, Kent CT11 9NY. Tel: 01628 825925
Hever Castle and Gardens – Nr Edenbridge, Kent TN8 7NG. Tel: 01732 861710
Leeds Castle and Gardens – Maidstone, Kent ME17 1PL. Tel: 01622 765400
Marle Place Garden and Gallery – Marle Place Road, Brenchley, Kent TN12 7HS. Tel: 01892 722304
Mount Ephraim Gardens – Staple Street, Hernhill, Nr Faversham, Kent ME13 9TX. Tel: 01227 751496
The New College of Cobham – Cobhambury Road, Cobham, Nr Gravesend, Kent DA12 3BG. Tel: 01474 812503
Riverhill Himalayan Gardens – Riverhill, Sevenoaks, Kent TN15 0RR. Tel: 01732 459777

Leicestershire

Stapleford Park – Stappleford Park, Nr Melton Mowbray, Leicestershire LE14 2EF. Tel: 01572 787000

London

18 Stafford Terrace – 18 Stafford Terrace, London W8 7BH. Tel: 0207 612 3306
Burgh House & Hampshire Museum – New End Square, Hampstead, London NW3 1LT. Tel: 020 7431 0144
Handel House Museum – 25 Brook Street, London W1K 4HB. Tel: 020 7495 1685
Keats House – Wentworth Place, Keats Grove, Hampstead, London NW3 2RR. Tel: 020 7794 6829
Leighton House – 12 Holland Park Road, London W14 8LZ. Tel: 020 7602 3316
Pitzhanger Manor House – Walpole Park, Mattock Lane, Ealing, London W5 5EQ. Tel: 020 8825 9803
St Paul's Cathedral – The Chapter House, St Paul's Churchyard, London EC4M 8AD. Tel: 020 7246 8350
Spencer House – 27 St. James's Place, London SW1A 1NR. Tel: 020 7514 1958
Syon Park – Syon Park, Brentford, London TW8 8JF. Tel: 020 8560 0882

Merseyside

Lady Lever Art Gallery – Port Sunlight Village, Wirral, Liverpool, Merseyside CH62 5EQ. Tel: 0151 478 4136
Meols Hall – Churchtown, Southport, Merseyside PR9 7LZ. Tel: 01704 228326
Sudley House – Mossley Hill Road, Aigburth, Liverpool, Merseyside L18 8BX. Tel: 0151 724 3245

Norfolk

Fairhaven Woodland and Water Garden – School Road, South Walsham, Norwich, Norfolk NR13 6DZ. Tel: 01603 270449
Mannington Hall – Saxthorpe, Norfolk NR11 7BB. Tel: 01263 584175 / 268444
South Elmham Hall – Hall Lane, St Cross, Harleston, Norfolk IP20 0PY. Tel: 01986 782526
Walsingham Abbey Grounds and Shirehall Museum – Common Place, Little Walsingham, Norfolk NR22 6BP. Tel: 01328 820510

Northumberland

Alnwick Castle – Alnwick, Northumberland NE66 1NQ. Tel: 01665 510777/ 511100

Bamburgh Castle – Bamburgh, Northumberland ME69 7DF. Tel: 01668 214208 / 214515
Chipchase Castle & Gardens – Wark on Tyne, Hexham, Northumberland NE48 3NT. Tel: 01434 230203

Oxfordshire

Blenheim Palace – Woodstock, Oxfordshire OX20 1PX. Tel: 0800 849 6500 (24 hour recorded message)
Broughton Castle – Banbury, Oxfordshire OX15 5EB. Tel: 01295 276070
Kingston Bagpuize House – Abingdon, Oxfordshire OX13 5AX. Tel: 01865 820259

We are pleased to feature over 170 places to visit during your stay at a Condé Nast Johansens Recommendation.
More information about these attractions, including opening times and entry fees, can be found on www.historichouses.co.uk

Mapledurham House & Watermill – Nr Reading, Oxfordshire RG4 7TR.
Tel: 01189 723350
Stonor Park – Nr Henley-on-Thames, Oxfordshire RG9 6HF. Tel: 01491 638587
Sulgrave Manor – Manor Road, Sulgrave, Banbury, Oxfordshire OX17 2SD.
Tel: 01295 760205
Wallingford Castle Gardens – Castle Street, Wallingford, Oxfordshire OX10 0AL.
Tel: 01491 835373

Rutland

Exton Park – Oakham, Rutland LE15 8AN. Tel: 01572 812208

Shropshire

Hodnet Hall Gardens – Hodnet, Market Drayton, Shropshire TF9 3NN.
Tel: 01630 685786
Ludlow Castle – Castle Square, Ludlow, Shropshire SY8 1AY. Tel: 01584 874465

Somerset

Glastonbury Abbey – Abbey Gatehouse, Magdalene Street, Glastonbury, Somerset BA6 9EL. Tel: 01458 832267
Great House Farm – Wells Road, Theale, Wedmore, Somerset BS28 4SJ.
Tel: 01934 713133
Hestercombe Gardens – Cheddon Fitzpaine, Taunton, Somerset TA2 8LG.
Tel: 01823 13923
Kentsford – Washford, Watchet, Somerset TA23 0JD. Tel: 01984 631307
No. 1 Royal Crescent – Bath, Somerset BA1 2LR. Tel: 01225 428126
Orchard Wyndham – Williton, Taunton, Somerset TA4 4HH. Tel: 01984 632309
Robin Hood's Hut – Halswell, Goathurst, Somerset. Tel: 01628 825925
Woodlands Castle – Woodlands, Ruishton, Taunton, Somerset TA3 5LU.
Tel: 01823 444955

Staffordshire

Whitmore Hall – Whitmore, Nr Newcastle-under-Lyme, Staffordshire ST5 5HW.
Tel: 01782 680478

Suffolk

Freston Tower – Near Ipswich, Suffolk IP9 1AD. Tel: 01628 825925
Kentwell Hall – Long Melford, Sudbury, Suffolk CO10 9BA. Tel: 01787 310207
Otley Hall – Hall Lane, Otley, Nr Ipswich, Suffolk IP6 9PA. Tel: 01473 890264

Surrey

Claremont Fan Court School – Claremont Drive, Esher, Surrey KT10 9LY.
Tel: 01372 473707
Guildford Castle – Castle Street, Guildford, Surrey GU1 3TU.
Tel: 01483 444751
Guildford House Gallery – 155 High Street, Guildford, Surrey GU1 3AJ.
Tel: 01483 444751
Painshill Park Landscape Garden – Portsmouth Road, Cobham, Surrey KT11 1JE.
Tel: 01932 868113
Ramster Gardens – Ramster, Chiddingfold, Surrey GU8 4SN. Tel: 01428 654167
Titsey Place and Gardens – Titsey, Oxted, Surrey RH8 0SD. Tel: 01273 475411

East Sussex

Bentley Wildfowl & Motor Museum – Halland, Nr Lewes, East Sussex BN8 5AF.
Tel: 01825 840573
Firle Place – Nr Lewes, East Sussex BN8 6LP. Tel: 01273 858307
Gardens and Grounds of Herstmonceux Castle – Hailsham, East Sussex
BN27 1RN. Tel: 01323 834444
Great Dixter House, Gardens & Nurseries – Great Dixter, Northiam, Rye,
East Sussex TN31 6PH. Tel: 01797 252878
Merriments Gardens – Hawkhurst Road, Hurst Green, East Sussex TN19 7RA.
Tel: 01580 860666
Pashley Manor Gardens – Ticehurst, East Sussex TN5 7HE. Tel: 01580 200888
Wilmington Priory – Wilmington, Nr Eastbourne, East Sussex BN26 5SW.
Tel: 01628 825925

West Sussex

Arundel Castle – Arundel, West Sussex BN18 9AB. Tel: 01903 882173
Borde Hill – Borde Hill Lane, Haywards Heath, West Sussex RH16 1XP.
Tel: 01444 450326
Cowdray – Visitor Centre, River Ground Stables, Midhurst, West Sussex GU29 9AL.
Tel: 01730 810781
Denmans Garden – Denmans Lane, Fontwell, West Sussex BN18 0SU.
Tel: 01243 542808
Goodwood House – Goodwood, Chichester, West Sussex PO18 0PX.
Tel: 01243 755000 / 755048
High Beeches Gardens – Handcross, West Sussex RH17 6HQ. Tel: 01444 400589
Parham House & Gardens – Parham Park, Storrington, Nr Pulborough, West
Sussex RH20 4HS. Tel: 01903 742021

Warwickshire

Arbury Hall – Nuneaton, Warwickshire CV10 7PT. Tel: 02476 382804

West Midlands

The Barber Institute of Fine Arts – University of Birmingham, Edgbaston,
Birmingham, West Midlands B15 2TS. Tel: 0121 414 7333
The Birmingham Botanical Gardens & Glasshouses – Westbourne Road,
Edgbaston, Birmingham, West Midlands B15 3TR. Tel: 0121 454 1860

Wiltshire

Iford Manor: The Peto Gardens – Bradford-on-Avon, Wiltshire BA15 2BA.
Tel: 01225 863 146

Worcestershire

Harvington Hall – Harvington, Kidderminster, Worcestershire DY10 4LR.
Tel: 01562 777846
Spetchley Park Gardens – Spetchley Park, Worcestershire WR5 1RS.
Tel: 01453 810303

North Yorkshire

Allerton Castle – Allerton Castle, Allerton Mauleverer, Knaresborough,
North Yorkshire HG5 0SE. Tel: 01423 330 927
Brockfield Hall – Warthill, York, North Yorkshire YO19 5XJ. Tel: 01904 489 362
The Forbidden Corner – Tupgill Park Estate, Coverham, Nr Middleham,
North Yorkshire DL8 4TJ. Tel: 01969 640638
Fountains Abbey and Studley Royal Water Garden – Ripon , Nr Harrogate,
North Yorkshire HG4 3DY. Tel: 01765 608888
Kiplin Hall – Nr Scorton, Richmond, North Yorkshire. Tel: 01748 818178
Newby Hall and Gardens – Ripon, North Yorkshire HG4 5AE. Tel: Information
Hotline: 0845 4504068Estate Office: 01423322583
Skipton Castle – Skipton, North Yorkshire BD23 1AW. Tel: 01756 792442

South Yorkshire

Epworth Old Rectory – Epworth, Doncaster, South Yorkshire DN9 1HX.
Tel: 01427 872268

West Yorkshire

Ledston Hall – Hall Lane, Ledston, Castleford, West Yorkshire WF10 2BB.
Tel: 01423 523 423
Shibden Hall – Listers Road, Halifax, West Yorkshire HX3 6XG. Tel: 01422 352246

Historic Houses, Castles & Gardens

We are pleased to feature over 170 places to visit during your stay at a Condé Nast Johansens Recommendation.
More information about these attractions, including opening times and entry fees, can be found on www.historichouses.co.uk

Northern Ireland

Co Down

Mount Stewart House and Gardens – Portaferry Road, Newtownards,
Co Down BT22 2AD. Tel: 028 4278 8387/028 4278 7817

Ireland

Cork

Bantry House & Garden – Bantry, Cork. Tel: 00 353 2 750 047
Blarney Castle, House and Garden – Blarney, Cork. Tel: 00 353 21 4385252

Kildare

The Irish National Stud – The Irish National Stud, Tully, kildare town , Kildare.
Tel: 00 353 45 521617

Offaly

Birr Castle Demesne – Birr, Offaly. Tel: 00 353 5791 20336

Wicklow

Mount Usher Gardens – Ashford, Wicklow. Tel: 00 353 40440205

Scotland

Aberdeenshire

Arbuthnott House – Arbuthnott, Laurencekirk, Aberdeenshire AB30 1PA.
Tel: 01561 320417
Duff House – Banff, Aberdeenshire AB45 3SX. Tel: 01261 818181
Provost Skene's House – Guestrow (off Broad Street), Aberdeen,
Aberdeenshire AB10 1AS. Tel: 01224 641086

Angus

Brechin Castle – Brechin, Angus DD9 6SG. Tel: 01356 624566

Ayrshire

Kelburn Castle and Country Centre – Kelburn, Fairlie (Nr Largs), Ayrshire
KA29 0BE. Tel: 01475 568685

North Ayrshire

Auchinleck House – Ochiltree, North Ayrshire. Tel: 01628 825925

Dumfries & Galloway

Ardwell Gardens – Ardwell House, Ardwell, Stranraer, Dumfries & Galloway
DG9 9LY. Tel: 01776 860227

**Castle Kennedy Gardens – The Estate Office, Rephad, Stranraer,
Dumfries & Galloway DG9 9BX. Tel: 01776 702 024**

Gilnockie Tower – 7 Riverside Park, , Canonbie , Dumfriesshire,
Dumfries & Galloway DG14 0UY. Tel: 01387 371876
Glenmalloch Lodge – Newton Stewart, Dumfries & Galloway. Tel: 01628 825925

East Lothian

Lennoxlove House – Lennoxlove Estate, Haddington, East Lothian EH41 4NZ.
Tel: 01620 823720

Highland

Clan Donald Skye – Armadale, Sleat, Isle of Skye, Highland IV45 8RS.
Tel: 01471 844305
Dunvegan Castle & Gardens – The MacLeod Estate Office, Dunvegan,
Isle of Skye, Highland IV55 8WF. Tel: (01470) 521206
Mount Stuart – Mount Stuart, Isle of Bute, Highland PA20 9LR. Tel: 01700 503877
Scone Palace – Scone, Perth, Perthshire, Highland PH2 6BD. Tel: 01738 552300

Scottish Borders

Abbotsford Gardens and Visitors Centre – Melrose, Roxburghshire,
Scottish Borders TD6 9BQ. Tel: 01896 752 043
Floors Castle – Kelso, Scottish Borders TD5 7SF. Tel: 01573 223333
Manderston – Duns, Berwickshire, Scottish Borders TD11 3PP. Tel: 01361 883 450
Mellerstain House – The Mellerstain Trust, Gordon, Berwickshire, Scottish Borders
TD3 6LG. Tel: 01573 410225
Paxton House, Gallery & Country Park – Paxton, Nr Berwick upon Tweed,
Scottish Borders TD15 1SZ. Tel: 01289 386291
Traquair House – Innerleithen, Peebles, Scottish Borders EH44 6PW.
Tel: 01896 830 323

Wales

Denbighshire

Dolbelydr – Trefnant, Denbighshire. Tel: 01628 825925

Flintshire

Golden Grove – Llanasa, Nr Holywell, Flintshire CH8 9NA. Tel: 01745 854452

Gwynedd

Portmeirion Village & Gardens – Portmeirion Village, Portmeirion, Gwynedd
LL48 6ER. Tel: (01766) 770000

Monmouthshire

Llanvihangel Court – Nr. Abergavenny, Monmouthshire NP7 8DH.
Tel: 01873 890 217 / 0208 947 9188
Usk Castle – Castle House, Monmouth Rd, Usk, Monmouthshire NP15 1SD.
Tel: 01291 672563

Newport

Tredegar House & Park – Newport NP10 8YW. Tel: 01633 815880

Pembrokeshire

St David's Cathedral – The Deanery, The Close, St Davids, Pembrokeshire SA62
6RH. Tel: 01437 720 202

Powys

The Judge's Lodging – Broad Street, Presteigne, Mid Wales, Powys LD8 2AD.
Tel: 01544 260650

France

Loire Valley

Château de Chenonceau – 37150 Chenonceaux, Loire Valley, France 37150.
Tel: 00 33 2 47 23 44 02

Normandy

Chateau de Martinvast and Floral Park – Domaine de Beaurepaire, 50690
Martinvast, Basse-Normandie, France 50690. Tel: 00 33 2 33 87 20 80

Hotels, Europe & The Mediterranean

All the properties listed below can be found in our Recommended Hotels & Spas, Europe & The Mediterranean 2012 Guide.

Austria

Hotel the Crystal .... Tirol ....**+43 5 256 6454**

Belgium

Manoir du Dragon ....Knokke~Heist ....+32 50 63 05 80
Hotel Damier Kortrijk ....Kortrijk ....+32 56 22 15 47
Hostellerie Ter Driezen............................Turnhout...................................+32 14 41 87 57

Channel Islands

The Atlantic Hotel .... Jersey ....**+44 1534 744101**

Croatia

Kazbek ....Dubrovnik ....+385 20 362 900
Villa Dubrovnik...Dubrovnik.............................. +385 20 500 300
Hotel Heritage Martinis Marchi ....Solta Island...............................+385 21 572 768

Egypt

Farah Nile Cruise....................................Luxor - Aswan ....+202 2418 5456/86

France

Hostellerie Les Bas Rupts Le Chalet Fleuri ....
.... Alsace~Lorraine...................+33 3 29 63 09 25
Hôtel à la Cour d'Alsace ....Alsace~Lorraine...................+33 3 88 95 07 00
Hôtel Les Têtes..Alsace~Lorraine...................+33 3 89 24 43 43
Romantik Hôtel le Maréchal.................Alsace~Lorraine...................+33 3 89 41 60 32
Domaine de Rochevilaine ....Brittany ....+33 2 97 41 61 61
Ti al Lannec & Spa ....Brittany ....+33 2 96 15 01 01
Abbaye de la Bussière ....Burgundy - Franche~Comté ....
....+33 3 80 49 02 29
Château Hôtel André Ziltener ....Burgundy - Franche~Comté ....
....+33 3 80 62 41 62
Ermitage de Corton..................................Burgundy - Franche~Comté ....
....+33 3 80 22 05 28
La Borde ....Burgundy - Franche~Comté ....
....+33 3 86 47 69 01
Château d'Etoges....................................Champagne~Ardenne ..... +33 3 26 59 30 08
Château de Fère ....Champagne~Ardenne ..... +33 3 23 82 21 13

Domaine du Château de Barive ... **Champagne~Ardenne.+33 3 23 22 15 15**
Hôtel Le Pinarello ....Corsica.....................................+33 4 95 71 44 39
Château Eza..Côte d'Azur.............................. +33 4 93 41 12 24
Hôtel Le Bailli de Suffren........................Côte d'Azur............................. +33 4 98 04 47 00
La Ferme d'Augustin................................Côte d'Azur.............................+33 4 94 55 97 00
La Villa Mauresque...................................Côte d'Azur.............................. +33 494 83 02 42
Le Spinaker ....Languedoc~Roussillon.....+33 4 66 53 36 37
Château de l'Abbaye...............................Loire Valley .... +33 251 56 17 56
Le Manoir Saint Thomas.........................Loire Valley ....+33 2 47 23 21 82
Château la Chenevière..............................Normandy ....+33 2 31 51 25 25
Carlton Hôtel..North~Picardy.......................+33 3 20 13 33 13

Hotels, Europe & The Mediterranean

All the properties listed below can be found in our Recommended Hotels & Spas, Europe & The Mediterranean 2012 Guide.

Hospes Lancaster ....Paris .... +33 1 40 76 40 76
Hotel Banke ....Paris .... +33 1 55 33 22 22
Hôtel de Buci ....Paris .... +33 1 55 42 74 74
Hôtel Duc de Saint~Simon ....Paris .... +33 1 44 39 20 20

Hotel La Belle Juliette.................... Paris ....+33 1 42 22 97 40
Hôtel San Régis ....Paris............................ +33 1 44 95 16 16
Les Pléiades ....Paris Region .... +33 1 60 66 40 25
Chalet Hôtel Kaya..............................Rhône~Alpes .... +33 4 79 41 42 00
Chalet Hôtel La Marmotte, Ski, Golf & Spa ....
....Rhône~Alpes .... +33 4 50 75 80 33
Château de Bagnols.........................Rhône~Alpes .... +33 4 74 71 40 00
Domaine des Avenières ....Rhône~Alpes .... +33 4 50 44 02 23
Le Beau Rivage................................Rhône~Alpes .... +33 4 74 56 82 82
Le Fer à Cheval................................Rhône~Alpes .... +33 4 50 21 30 39
Le Portetta......................................Rhône~Alpes .... +33 4 79 08 01 47
Château de Mirambeau ....South West .... +33 5 46 04 91 20
Hôtel du Palais................................South West .... +33 5 59 41 64 00

Villa La Tosca................................... South West ....+33 556 60 29 86

Germany

Aspria Spa + Sporting Club + Hotel..Berlin.................................. +49 30 890 68 88 68

Great Britain

Beaufort House ....England .... +44 20 7584 2600
The French Horn ....England .... +44 1189 692 204

The May Fair .... England .... +44 20 7769 3046
The Mayflower Hotel ....England ....+44 20 7370 0991
The New Linden Hotel ....England ....+44 20 7221 4321
Twenty Nevern Square ....England ....+44 20 7565 9555

Greece

Argentikon Luxury Suites ....Chios ....+30 22710 33111
Domes of Elounda, All Suites and Villas Spa Resort ....
....Crete..........................+30 2310 810624
Pleiades Luxurious Villas ....Crete ....+30 2310 810624
Apanema Resort................................Mykonos ....+30 22890 28590

Tharroe of Mykonos .... Mykonos........................+30 22890 27370
Naxian Collection Luxury Villas and Suites ....
....Naxos...........................+30 228 502 4300

Hotels, Europe & The Mediterranean

All the properties listed below can be found in our Recommended Hotels & Spas, Europe & The Mediterranean 2012 Guide.

Petra Hotel & Suites......................Patmos......................+30 22470 34020
9 Muses Santorini Resort ....Santorini....................+30 228 608 1781

Andronis Luxury Suites .... Santorini................. +30 22860 72041/2/3
Astra Suites ....Santorini...........................+30 22860 23641
Petit Palace..Santorini.................. +30 22860 23949/23944
Santorini Icons Hotel ....Santorini........................+30 228 602 8950
Timedrops Santorini ....Santorini...........................+30 2 28 60 83 282
White Santorini ....Santorini...................................+30 22860 25257
Lesante Hotel & Spa ....Zakynthos...........................+30 2 69 50 41 330

Italy

Hotel Punta Tragara .... Campania .... +39 081 8370844
Hotel Posta (Historical Residence) .....Emilia Romagna.................+39 05 22 43 29 44
Palazzo Dalla Rosa Prati ....Emilia Romagna..................+39 0521 386 429
Buonanotte Garibaldi ....Lazio.........................+39 06 58 330 733
Casa Montani - Luxury Town House .Lazio....................................+39 06 3260 0421
Hotel dei Borgognoni.............................Lazio.............................+39 06 6994 1505
Hotel dei Consoli ....Lazio.................................+39 0668 892 972
La Posta Vecchia ....Lazio.................... +39 0699 49501

Palazzo Manfredi ....Lazio..............................+39 06 77591380
Residenza Napoleone III......................Lazio......................+39 3477 337 098
Villa Spalletti Trivelli..............................Lazio..............................+39 06 48907934
Abbadia San Giorgio - Historical Residence ....
                                                   Liguria ....+39 0185 491119
Eight Hotel Paraggi ....Liguria ....+39 0185 289961
Eight Hotel Portofino............................Liguria .... +39 0185 26991
Grand Hotel Bristol Resort & Spa.......Liguria ....+ 39 0185 273 313
Grand Hotel Diana Majestic.................Liguria ....+39 0183 402 727
Grand Hotel Miramare ....Liguria ....+39 0185 287013
Hotel Punta Est...Liguria .... +39 019 600611
Hotel Vis à Vis ....Liguria .... +39 0185 42661
Bagni di Bormio Spa Resort...............Lombardy ....+39 0342 910131
Camperio House Suites and Apartments..
                                                   Lombardy ....+39 02 303 22800
Grand Hotel Gardone Riviera..............Lombardy .... +39 0365 20261
Hotel Bellerive ....Lombardy ....+39 0365 520 410
Hotel de la Ville & La Villa ....Lombardy ....+39 039 39421
L'Albereta ....Lombardy ....+39 030 7760 550
Excelsior Hotel ....Marche ....+39 0721 630011
Albergo L'Ostelliere ....Piemonte ....+39 0143 607 801
Relais Bella Rosina...............................Piemonte...............................+39 011 9233600
Relais San Maurizio..............................Piemonte..............................+39 0141 841900
Hotel Lucrezia ....Sardinia ....+39 0783 412078
Hotel Relais Villa del Golfo & Spa.........Sardinia.........+ 39 0789 892091
Petra Segreta Resort & SPA ....Sardinia ....+39 0789 187 6441
Villa Las Tronas Hotel & Spa ....Sardinia .... +39 079 981 818

**Baia Taormina Grand Palace Hotels & Spa ....
                                                   Sicily............................... +39 0942 756292**
Donna Carmela Resort ....Sicily .... +39 095 809383
Hotel Signum..Sicily........................+39 090 9844222
Hotel Villa Ducale ....Sicily .... +39 0942 28153
Locanda Don Serafino ....Sicily ....+39 0932 220065
Palazzo Failla Hotel ....Sicily ....+39 0932 941059
Villa Carlotta ....Sicily ....+39 0942 626058
Castel Fragsburg.....................................Trentino - Alto Adige / Dolomites....................
                                                   +39 0473 244071
Du Lac et Du Parc Grand Resort.........Trentino - Alto Adige / Dolomites....................
                                                   +39 0464 566600
feldmilla. designhotel ....Trentino - Alto Adige / Dolomites....................
                                                   +39 0474 677100
GranPanorama Hotel Miramonti........Trentino - Alto Adige / Dolomites....................
                                                   +39 0473 27 9335

Hotels, Europe & The Mediterranean

All the properties listed below can be found in our Recommended Hotels & Spas, Europe & The Mediterranean 2012 Guide.

Hotel Ciasa Salares...................................Trentino - Alto Adige / Dolomites..................
+39 0471 849445

Hotel Gardena Grödnerhof.......... Trentino - Alto Adige / Dolomites.............
+39 0471 796 315

Lido Palace...Trentino - Alto Adige / Dolomites..................
+39 0464 021899

Parkhotel Holzner ....Trentino - Alto Adige / Dolomites..................
+39 0471 345 231

Albergo Pietrasanta - Palazzo Barsanti Bonetti ....
Tuscany ....+39 0584 793 727

Albergo Villa Casanova .... Tuscany..........................+39 0583 369000

Borgo Scopeto Relais ....Tuscany........................+39 0577 320001

Castello del Nero Hotel & Spa.............Tuscany........................+ 39 055 806 470

Country House Casa Cornacchi ....Tuscany........................+ 39 055 998229

Country Relais Villa L'Olmo...................Tuscany........................+39 055 23 11 311

Granduomo Charming Accommodation...
Tuscany ....+39 055 267 0004

Hotel Byron...Tuscany........................+39 0584 787 052

Hotel Plaza e de Russie ....Tuscany........................+ 39 0584 44449

Hotel Tornabuoni Beacci.........................Tuscany........................+ 39 055 212645

Il Bottaccio di Montignoso....................Tuscany........................+39 0585 340031

Il Pellicano Hotel ....Tuscany........................+39 0564 858111

L'Andana..Tuscany........................+39 0564 944 800

Lucignanello Bandini (Borgo Storico) ....
Tuscany ....+39 0577 803 068

Marignolle Relais & Charme ....Tuscany........................+39 055 228 6910

Monsignor Della Casa Country Resort & Spa...
Tuscany ....+ 39 055 840 821

Palazzo Carletti..Tuscany........................+39 0578 756080

Palazzo Magnani Feroni - all-suites florence ....
Tuscany ....+39 055 2399544

Palazzo San Lorenzo ....Tuscany........................+39 0577 923675

Petriolo Spa Resort ....Tuscany........................+39 0564 9091

Relais Borgo San Felice ....Tuscany........................+39 0577 3964

Relais la Suvera (Dimora Storica)........Tuscany........................+39 0577 960 300

Relais Villa Belpoggio (Historical House)..
Tuscany ....+39 055 9694411

Residenza del Moro...................................Tuscany........................+ 39 055 290884

Tenuta San Pietro Luxury Hotel & Restaurant..
Tuscany ....+39 0583 926676

Tombolo Talasso Resort..........................Tuscany........................+39 0565 74530

Villa Armena, Relais & Beauty Farm....Tuscany........................+39 331 61 88 767

Villa Campestri Olive Oil Resort ....Tuscany........................+39 055 849 0107

Villa Curina Resort ....Tuscany........................+39 0577 355630

Villa le Barone ....Tuscany........................+ 39 055 852621

Castello di Petroia ....Umbria.........................+39 075 92 02 87

L'Antico Forziere Restaurant & Country Inn ....
Umbria.........................+39 075 972 4314

Romantik Hotel Jolanda Sport ....Valle d'Aosta ....+39 0125 366 140

Albergo Quattro Fontane - Residenza d'Epoca ....
Veneto..........................+39 041 526 0227

Ca Maria Adele ....Veneto..........................+39 041 52 03 078

Ca' Sagredo Hotel ....Veneto..........................+39 041 2413111

Color Hotel style & design......................Veneto..........................+39 045 621 0857

Hotel Caesius Thermae & SPA Resort ....
Veneto..........................+39 045 7219100

Locanda San Vigilio ....Veneto..........................+39 045 725 66 88

Londra Palace ....Veneto..........................+39 041 5200533

Palazzo Selvadego ....Veneto..........................+ 39 041 5200211

Park Hotel Brasilia..........................Veneto ....+39 0421 380851

Relais Corte Guastalla ....Veneto..........................+39 045 6095614

Relais la Magioca......................................Veneto..........................+39 045 600 0167

Villa Cordevigo...Veneto..........................+39 045 723 5287

Hotels, Europe & The Mediterranean

All the properties listed below can be found in our Recommended Hotels & Spas, Europe & The Mediterranean 2012 Guide.

Morocco

Kasbah Du Toubkal.................................High Atlas Mountains.......+212 524 48 56 11
Dar Azawad ....M'hamid..................................+212 524 84 87 30

Riad Enija .... Marrakech - Medina ...+212 5 24 44 09 26
La Gazelle d'Or...Taroudant ....+212 528 852 039

The Netherlands

Ambassade Hotel.......................................Amsterdam .... +31 20 5550 222

Portugal

Longevity Wellness Resort Monchique...
                                                 Algarve...................................+351 282 240 110
Tivoli Marina Vilamoura........................Algarve ....+351 289 303 303
Tivoli Victoria...Algarve ....+351 289 31 7000
Altis Belém Hotel & Spa.........................Lisbon & Tagus Valley ....+351 210 400 200

As Janelas Verdes............................. Lisbon & Tagus Valley +351 21 39 68 143
Heritage Av Liberdade.............................Lisbon & Tagus Valley ....+351 213 404 040

Hotel Albatroz ....Lisbon & Tagus Valley ....+351 21 484 73 80
Hotel Britania ....Lisbon & Tagus Valley ....+351 21 31 55 016
Lisboa Plaza Hotel ....Lisbon & Tagus Valley ....+351 213 218 218
Palácio Estoril, Hotel, Golf & Spa ....Lisbon & Tagus Valley ....+351 21 464 80 00
Solar do Castelo ....Lisbon & Tagus Valley ....+351 218 806 050
Tivoli Palácio de Seteais.........................Lisbon & Tagus Valley ....+351 219 233 200
The Yeatman Hotel ....Oporto & Northern Portugal............................
                                                 +351 22 013 3100

Spain

Barceló la Bobadilla...................................Andalucía................................. +34 958 32 18 61
DDG Luxury Retreat...................................Andalucía................................. +34 629 657 203

Don Carlos Leisure Resort & Spa .. Andalucía ....+34 952 76 88 00
El Ladrón de Agua.......................................Andalucía................................. +34 958 21 50 40
Gran Meliá Colón...Andalucía................................. +34 954 50 55 99
Gran Meliá Don Pepe Hotel ....Andalucía................................. +34 952 770 300
Hacienda Benazuza......................................Andalucía................................. +34 955 70 33 44
Hospes las Casas del Rey de Baeza....Andalucía................................. +34 954 561 496
Hospes Palacio de los Patos................Andalucía................................. +34 958 535 790
Hospes Palacio del Bailío ....Andalucía................................. +34 957 498 993
La Almoraima Hotel ....Andalucía................................. +34 956 693 002

Vincci Selección Estrella del Mar .. Andalucía ....+34 951 053 970
Vincci Seleccion Posada del Patio ......Andalucía................................. +34 951 001 020
Blau Porto Petro Beach Resort & Spa ..Balearic Islands....................+34 971 648 282
Can Lluc...Balearic Islands..................... +34 971 198 673
Cas Gasi ....Balearic Islands..................... +34 971 197 700
Cases de Son Barbassa............................Balearic Islands..................... +34 971 565 776

Hotels, Europe & The Mediterranean

All the properties listed below can be found in our Recommended Hotels & Spas, Europe & The Mediterranean 2012 Guide.

Gran Hotel Son Net ....Balearic Islands....................... +34 971 14 70 00
Hospes Maricel...Balearic Islands....................... +34 971 707 744

Hotel Sant Joan de Binissaida ...... Balearic Islands..............+34 971 35 55 98
Hotel Ses Pitreras.............................Balearic Islands .... +34 971 345 000
Son Granot..Balearic Islands .... +34 971 355 555
Gran Hotel Atlantis Bahía Real.............Canary Islands....................... +34 928 53 64 44
Gran Hotel Bahía del Duque Resort ..Canary Islands....................... +34 922 746 900
Hotel Botánico & The Oriental Spa Garden...
                                                Canary Islands....................... +34 922 38 14 00
Vincci Selección La Plantacion del Sur..
                                                Canary Islands....................... +34 922 717 773
La Almazara de Valdeverdeja...............Castilla~La Mancha .... +34 925 454 804
Dolce Sitges...Cataluña .... +34 938 109 000

Hotel 1898 .... Cataluña ....+34 93 552 95 52
Hotel Bagués...Cataluña .... +34 93 34 35 000
Hotel Casa Fuster..................................Cataluña .... +34 93 255 30 00

Hotel Duquesa de Cardona ....Cataluña .... +34 93 268 90 90
Hotel Guitart Monterrey ....Cataluña .... +34 972 34 60 54
Hotel Omm ....Cataluña .... +34 93 445 40 00
Hotel Rigat Park & Spa Beach Hotel ..Cataluña .... +34 972 36 52 00
Hotel Santa Marta..................................Cataluña .... +34 972 364 904
Hotel Vistabella ....Cataluña .... +34 972 25 62 00
Hotel Etxegana Charming Hotel & Spa ....
                                                País Vasco................................. +34 946 338 448
Barceló Asia Gardens Hotel & Thai Spa..
                                                Valencia..................................... +34 966 818 400
El Rodat Hotel ....Valencia..................................... +34 966 470 710
Hotel Termas Marinas el Palasiet ....Valencia..................................... +34 964 300 250
Hotel Villa Marisol ....Valencia..................................... +34 96 587 57 00

Switzerland

Hotel Guarda Golf..................................Crans~Montana...................... +41 27 486 2000
LeCrans Hotel & Spa.............................Crans~Montana...................... +41 27 486 60 60

Park Hotel Weggis......................... Weggis ....+41 41 392 05 05
CERVO Mountain Boutique Resort....Zermatt.................................... +41 27 968 12 12

Turkey

Cornelia Diamond Golf Resort and Spa ....
                                                Antalya...................................... +90 242 710 1600
Kempinski Hotel Barbaros Bay ....Bodrum....................................+90 252 311 03 03
Gardens of Babylon Suites & Residence...
                                                Bodrum - Turgutreis ....+90 252 382 8217
Argos in Cappadocia ....Cappadocia - Uçhisar..........+90 384 2193130
Sacred House ....Cappadocia - Ürgüp..........+90 384 341 7102
A'jia Hotel...Istanbul....................................+90 216 413 9300
Neorion Hotel...Istanbul....................................+90 212 527 9090
Sumahan On The Water ....Istanbul....................................+90 216 422 8000
Villa Mahal...Kalkan......................................+90 242 844 32 68
Golden Key Bördübet............................Marmaris.................................+90 252 436 92 30

Hotels - The Americas

Properties listed below can be found in our Recommended Hotels, Inns, Resorts & Spas – The Americas, Atlantic, Caribbean & Pacific 2012 Guide

Recommendations in Canada — p168

Recommendations in México — p168

Recommendations in USA — p170

Recommendations in Central Amercia — p174

Recommendations in South America — p176

Recommendations in the Atlantic — p180

Recommendations in the Caribbean — p180

Recommendations in the Pacific — p182

CANADA - BRITISH COLUMBIA (SONORA ISLAND)

Sonora Resort

Sonora Island, British Columbia

Tel: +1 604 233 0460
www.condenastjohansens.com/sonoraresort

CANADA - BRITISH COLUMBIA (SOOKE)

Sooke Harbour House

1528 Whiffen Spit Road, Sooke, British Columbia
V9Z 0T4

Tel: +1 250 642 3421
www.condenastjohansens.com/sookeharbour

CANADA - BRITISH COLUMBIA (TOFINO)

Clayoquot Wilderness Resort

P.O. Box 130, Tofino, British Columbia V0R 2Z0

Tel: +1 250 726 8235
www.condenastjohansens.com/clayoquot

CANADA - BRITISH COLUMBIA (TOFINO)

Wickaninnish Inn

Osprey Lane at Chesterman Beach, Tofino, British
Columbia V0R 2Z0

Tel: +1 250 725 3100
www.condenastjohansens.com/wickaninnish

CANADA - BRITISH COLUMBIA (VANCOUVER)

Loden Hotel

1177 Melville Street, Vancouver, British Columbia
V6E 0A3

Tel: +1 604 669 5060
www.condenastjohansens.com/theloden

CANADA - BRITISH COLUMBIA (VANCOUVER)

Wedgewood Hotel & Spa

845 Hornby Street, Vancouver, British Columbia
V6Z 1V1

Tel: +1 604 689 7777
www.condenastjohansens.com/wedgewoodbc

CANADA - BRITISH COLUMBIA (VICTORIA)

The Magnolia Hotel & Spa

623 Courtney Street, Victoria, British Columbia
V8W 1B8

Tel: +1 250 381 0999
www.condenastjohansens.com/magnoliahotel

CANADA - NOVA SCOTIA (EAST KEMPTVILLE)

Trout Point Lodge of Nova Scotia

189 Trout Point Road, Off the East Branch Road and
Highway 203, East Kemptville, Nova Scotia B0W 1Y0

Tel: +1 902 761 2142
www.condenastjohansens.com/troutpoint

CANADA - ONTARIO (NIAGARA-ON-THE-LAKE)

Harbour House

85 Melville Street, Box 760, Niagara-on-the-Lake,
Ontario L0S 1J0

Tel: +1 905 468 4683
www.condenastjohansens.com/harbourhouseca

CANADA - ONTARIO (TORONTO)

Windsor Arms

18 St. Thomas Street, Toronto, Ontario M5S 3E7

Tel: +1 416 971 9666
www.condenastjohansens.com/windsorarms

CANADA - QUÉBEC (MONT-TREMBLANT)

Hôtel Quintessence

3004 chemin de la chapelle, Mont-Tremblant, Québec
J8E 1E1

Tel: +1 819 425 3400
www.condenastjohansens.com/quintessence

CANADA - QUÉBEC (NORTH HATLEY)

Manoir Hovey

575 Hovey Road, North Hatley, Québec J0B 2C0

Tel: +1 819 842 2421
www.condenastjohansens.com/manoirhovey

MÉXICO - GUANAJUATO (GUANAJUATO)

Villa Maria Cristina

Paseo de La Presa de la Olla No. 76 Centro, Guanajuato,
Guanajuato 36000

Tel: +52 473 731 2182
www.condenastjohansens.com/villamariacristina

Properties listed below can be found in our Recommended Hotels, Inns, Resorts & Spas – The Americas, Atlantic, Caribbean & Pacific 2012 Guide

MÉXICO - GUERRERO (ACAPULCO)

Las Brisas Acapulco

Carretera Escenica 5255, Acapulco, Guerrero 39867

Tel: +52 744 469 6900
www.condenastjohansens.com/brisasacapulco

MÉXICO - MÉXICO (VALLE DE BRAVO)

Hotel Rodavento

Km.3.5 Carretera Valle de Bravo -Los Saucos, Valle de Bravo, México 51200

Tel: +52 726 251 4182
www.condenastjohansens.com/rodavento

MÉXICO - GUERRERO (IXTAPA - ZIHUATANEJO)

Loma del Mar

Ixtapa - Zihuatanejo, Guerrero 40884

Tel: +52 755 555 0460
www.condenastjohansens.com/lomadelmar

MÉXICO - MORELOS (CUERNAVACA)

Las Mañanitas Hotel, Garden Restaurant & Spa

Ricardo Linares 107, Centro 62000, Cuernavaca, Morelos

Tel: +52 777 362 00 00
www.condenastjohansens.com/lasmananitas

MÉXICO - JALISCO (COSTALEGRE - PUERTO VALLARTA)

Las Alamandas Resort

Carretera Barra de Navidad - Puerto Vallarta km 83.5, Col. Quemaro, Jalisco 48850

Tel: +52 322 285 5500
www.condenastjohansens.com/alamandas

MÉXICO - MORELOS (TEPOZTLÁN)

Hostal de La Luz

Carretera Federal Tepoztlán, Amatlan Km. 4, Tepoztlán, Morelos 62524

Tel: +1 739 393 3076
www.condenastjohansens.com/hostaldelaluz

MÉXICO - JALISCO (GUADALAJARA)

Del Carmen Concept Hotel

Jacobo Galvez No.45, Zona Centro, Guadalajara, Jalisco 44100

Tel: +52 33 3614 2640/9875
www.condenastjohansens.com/delcarmen

MÉXICO - NAYARIT (PUNTA DE MITA)

Casa Papelillos

Punta de Mita, Nayarit 63734

Tel: +1 214 924 6427
www.condenastjohansens.com/casapapelillos

MÉXICO - JALISCO (JOCOTEPEC)

El Chante Spa Hotel

Rivera del Lago 170-1, El Chante, Jocotepec, Jalisco 45825

Tel: +52 387 763 26 08
www.condenastjohansens.com/elchantespa

MÉXICO - NAYARIT (PUNTA DE MITA)

Imanta Resorts Punta de Mita, México

Montenahuac Lote-L, Higuera Blanca, Nayarit CP63734

Tel: +52 329 298 4200
www.condenastjohansens.com/imantaresorts

MÉXICO - JALISCO (PUERTO VALLARTA)

Casa Velas

Pelicanos 311, Fracc. Marina Vallarta, Puerto Vallarta, Jalisco 48354

Tel: +52 322 226 6688
www.condenastjohansens.com/casavelas

MÉXICO - OAXACA (HUATULCO)

Casa Bichu

Estacahuite Bay, Puerto Ángel, Oaxaca 70902

Tel: +52 958 58 434 89
www.condenastjohansens.com/casabichu

MÉXICO - JALISCO (PUERTO VALLARTA)

Garza Blanca Preserve Resort & Spa

Km. 7.5 Carretera a Barra de Navidad, Puerto Vallarta, Jalisco 48390

Tel: +52 322 176 0700
www.condenastjohansens.com/garzablancaresort

MÉXICO - QUINTANA ROO (CANCÚN - PUERTO MORELOS)

Ceiba del Mar Beach & Spa Resort

Costera Norte Lte. 1, S.M. 10, MZ. 26, Puerto Morelos, Quintana Roo 77580

Tel: +1 877 545 6221
www.condenastjohansens.com/ceibadelmar

MÉXICO - MÉXICO (NUEVO VALLARTA - RIVIERA NAYARIT)

Villa La Estancia Riviera Nayarit

Paseo Cocoteros 750 Sur, Condominio Maestro Flamingos, Nuevo Vallarta, Riviera Nayarit 63732

Tel: +52 322 226 9700
www.condenastjohansens.com/villalaestancia

MÉXICO - QUINTANA ROO (PLAYA DEL CARMEN)

Le Reve Hotel & Spa

Playa Xcalacoco Fraccion 2A, Playa del Carmen, Quintana Roo 77710

Tel: +52 984 109 5660/5661
www.condenastjohansens.com/hotellereve

Hotels - The Americas

Properties listed below can be found in our Recommended Hotels, Inns, Resorts & Spas – The Americas, Atlantic, Caribbean & Pacific 2012 Guide

MÉXICO - VERACRUZ (JALCOMULCO)

Rio y Montaña

Domicilio Conocido, Col. Centro, Jalcomulco,
Veracruz 9400

Tel: +52 279 8323 596
www.condenastjohansens.com/rioymontana

U.S.A. - CALIFORNIA (BIG SUR)

Post Ranch Inn

Highway 1, P.O. Box 219, Big Sur, California 93920

Tel: +1 831 667 2200
www.condenastjohansens.com/postranchinn

MÉXICO - YUCATÁN (MÉRIDA)

Hacienda Xcanatún - Casa de Piedra

Calle 20 S/N, Comisaría Xcanatún, Km. 12 Carretera
Mérida - Progreso, Mérida, Yucatán 97302

Tel: +52 999 930 2140
www.condenastjohansens.com/xcanatun

U.S.A. - CALIFORNIA (BIG SUR)

Ventana Inn and Spa

48123 Highway One, Big Sur, California 93920

Tel: +1 831 667 2331
www.condenastjohansens.com/ventanainn

U.S.A. - ARIZONA (GREER)

Hidden Meadow Ranch

620 County Road 1325, Greer, Arizona 85927

Tel: +1 928 333 1000
www.condenastjohansens.com/hiddenmeadow

U.S.A. - CALIFORNIA (CALISTOGA)

Cottage Grove Inn

1711 Lincoln Avenue, Calistoga, California 94515

Tel: +1 707 942 8400/2657
www.condenastjohansens.com/cottagegrove

U.S.A. - ARIZONA (PARADISE VALLEY)

The Hermosa Inn

5532 North Palo Cristi Road, Paradise Valley,
Arizona 85253

Tel: +1 602 955 8614
www.condenastjohansens.com/hermosa

U.S.A. - CALIFORNIA (CARMEL-BY-THE-SEA)

L'Auberge Carmel

Monte Verde at Seventh, Carmel-by-the-Sea,
California 93921

Tel: +1 831 624 8578
www.condenastjohansens.com/laubergecarmel

U.S.A. - ARIZONA (PARADISE VALLEY - SCOTTSDALE)

Sanctuary on Camelback Mountain

5700 East McDonald Drive, Scottsdale, Arizona 85253

Tel: +1 480 948 2100
www.condenastjohansens.com/sanctuaryaz

U.S.A. - CALIFORNIA (CARMEL-BY-THE-SEA)

Tradewinds Carmel

Mission Street at Third Avenue, Carmel-by-the-Sea,
California 93921

Tel: +1 831 624 2776
www.condenastjohansens.com/tradewinds

U.S.A. - ARIZONA (TUCSON)

Hacienda del Sol Guest Ranch Resort

5501 N. Hacienda del Sol Road, Tucson, Arizona 85718

Tel: +1 520 299 1501
www.condenastjohansens.com/haciendadelsol

U.S.A. - CALIFORNIA (CARMEL VALLEY)

Bernardus Lodge

415 Carmel Valley Road, Carmel Valley, California 93924

Tel: +1 831 658 3400
www.condenastjohansens.com/bernardus

U.S.A. - ARIZONA (TUCSON)

Tanque Verde Ranch

14301 East Speedway Boulevard, Tucson,
Arizona 85748

Tel: +1 520 296 6275
www.condenastjohansens.com/tanqueverde

U.S.A. - CALIFORNIA (HEALDSBURG)

Hotel Les Mars

27 North Street, Healdsburg, California 95448

Tel: +1 707 433 4211
www.condenastjohansens.com/lesmarshotel

U.S.A. - ARIZONA (TUCSON)

Westward Look Resort

245 E. Ina Road, Tucson, Arizona 85704

Tel: +1 520 297 1151
www.condenastjohansens.com/westwardlook

U.S.A. - CALIFORNIA (LA JOLLA)

Grande Colonial Hotel La Jolla

910 Prospect Street, La Jolla, California 92037

Tel: +1 855 380 4454
www.condenastjohansens.com/gclj

Properties listed below can be found in our Recommended Hotels, Inns, Resorts & Spas – The Americas, Atlantic, Caribbean & Pacific 2012 Guide

U.S.A. - CALIFORNIA (LA JOLLA)

Hotel Parisi

1111 Prospect Street, La Jolla, California 92037

Tel: +1 858 454 1511
www.condenastjohansens.com/hotelparisi

U.S.A. - CALIFORNIA (SAN FRANCISCO BAY AREA)

Inn Above Tide

30 El Portal, Sausalito, California 94965

Tel: +1 415 332 9535
www.condenastjohansens.com/innabovetide

U.S.A. - CALIFORNIA (LAKE TAHOE)

PlumpJack Squaw Valley Inn

1920 Squaw Valley Road, Olympic Valley,
California 96146

Tel: +1 530 583 1576
www.condenastjohansens.com/plumpjack

U.S.A. - CALIFORNIA (YOUNTVILLE)

Bardessono

6526 Yount Street, Yountville, California 94599

Tel: +1 707 204 6000
www.condenastjohansens.com/bardessono

U.S.A. - CALIFORNIA (MENDOCINO)

The Stanford Inn By The Sea

Coast Highway One & Comptche-Ukiah Road,
Mendocino, California 95460

Tel: +1 707 937 5615
www.condenastjohansens.com/stanfordinn

U.S.A. - COLORADO (DENVER)

Castle Marne Bed & Breakfast Inn

1572 Race Street, Denver, Colorado 80206

Tel: +1 303 331 0621
www.condenastjohansens.com/castlemarne

U.S.A. - CALIFORNIA (MONTEREY)

Old Monterey Inn

500 Martin Street, Monterey, California 93940

Tel: +1 831 375 8284
www.condenastjohansens.com/oldmontereyinn

U.S.A. - COLORADO (ESTES PARK)

Taharaa Mountain Lodge

P.O. Box 2586, 3110 So. St. Vrain, Estes Park,
Colorado 80517

Tel: +1 970 577 0098
www.condenastjohansens.com/taharaa

U.S.A. - CALIFORNIA (NAPA)

1801 First Inn

1801 First Street, Napa, California 94559

Tel: +1 707 224 3739
www.condenastjohansens.com/1801first

U.S.A. - COLORADO (STEAMBOAT SPRINGS)

Vista Verde Guest Ranch

P.O. Box 770465, Steamboat Springs, Colorado 80477

Tel: +1 970 879 3858
www.condenastjohansens.com/vistaverderanch

U.S.A. - CALIFORNIA (NAPA)

Milliken Creek Inn & Spa

1815 Silverado Trail, Napa, California 94558

Tel: +1 707 255 1197
www.condenastjohansens.com/milliken

U.S.A. - COLORADO (TELLURIDE)

Hotel Columbia

301 West San Juan Avenue, Telluride, Colorado 81435

Tel: +1 970 728 0660/6294
www.condenastjohansens.com/columbiatelluride

U.S.A. - CALIFORNIA (NAPA)

White House Inn & Spa

443 Brown Street, Napa, California 94559

Tel: +1 707 254 9301
www.condenastjohansens.com/whitehousenapa

U.S.A. - COLORADO (TELLURIDE)

lumiére Telluride

118 Lost Creek Lane, Telluride, Colorado 81435

Tel: +1 970 369 0400
www.condenastjohansens.com/lumiere

U.S.A. - CALIFORNIA (RANCHO SANTA FE)

The Inn at Rancho Santa Fe

5951 Linea del Cielo, Rancho Santa Fe, California 92067

Tel: +1 858 756 1131
www.condenastjohansens.com/ranchosantafe

U.S.A. - COLORADO (VAIL)

The Sebastian - Vail

16 Vail Road, Vail, Colorado 81657

Tel: +1 970 331 0655
www.condenastjohansens.com/thesebastianvail

Hotels - The Americas

Properties listed below can be found in our Recommended Hotels, Inns, Resorts & Spas – The Americas, Atlantic, Caribbean & Pacific 2012 Guide

U.S.A. - COLORADO (VAIL)

Vail Mountain Lodge & Spa

352 East Meadow Drive, Vail, Colorado 81657

Tel: +1 970 476 0700

www.condenastjohansens.com/vailmountain

U.S.A. - FLORIDA (MIAMI BEACH)

The Setai South Beach

2001 Collins Avenue, Miami Beach, Florida 33139

Tel: +1 305 520 6000/6110

www.condenastjohansens.com/setai

U.S.A. - DELAWARE (REHOBOTH BEACH)

Boardwalk Plaza Hotel

Olive Avenue & The Boardwalk, Rehoboth Beach, Delaware 19971

Tel: +1 302 227 7169

www.condenastjohansens.com/boardwalkplaza

U.S.A. - GEORGIA (CUMBERLAND ISLAND)

Greyfield Inn

Cumberland Island, Georgia

Tel: +1 904 261 6408

www.condenastjohansens.com/greyfieldinn

U.S.A. - DELAWARE (WILMINGTON)

Inn at Montchanin Village & Spa

Route 100 & Kirk Road, Montchanin, Wilmington, Delaware 19710

Tel: +1 302 888 2133

www.condenastjohansens.com/montchanin

U.S.A. - ILLINOIS (CHICAGO)

Trump International Hotel & Tower® Chicago

401 North Wabash Avenue, Chicago, Illinois 60611

Tel: +1 312 588 8000

www.condenastjohansens.com/trumpchicago

U.S.A. - DISTRICT OF COLUMBIA (WASHINGTON D.C.)

The Hay-Adams

Sixteenth & H. Streets N.W., Washington D.C., District of Columbia 20006

Tel: +1 202 638 6600

www.condenastjohansens.com/hayadams

U.S.A. - MAINE (CAMDEN)

Camden Harbour Inn

83 Bayview Street, Camden, Maine 04843

Tel: +1 207 236 4200

www.condenastjohansens.com/camdenharbourinn

U.S.A. - FLORIDA (BAL HARBOUR, MIAMI BEACH)

ONE Bal Harbour

10295 Collins Avenue, Bal Harbour, Florida 33154

Tel: +1 305 455 5400/5459

www.condenastjohansens.com/onebalharbour

U.S.A. - MAINE (KENNEBUNK BEACH)

The White Barn Inn & Spa

37 Beach Avenue, Kennebunk Beach, Maine 04043

Tel: +1 207 967 2321

www.condenastjohansens.com/whitebarninn

U.S.A. - FLORIDA (FISHER ISLAND)

Fisher Island Club & Resort

One Fisher Island Drive, Fisher Island, Florida 33109

Tel: +1 305 535 6000

www.condenastjohansens.com/fisherisland

U.S.A. - MAINE (PORTLAND)

Portland Harbor Hotel

468 Fore Street, Portland, Maine 04101

Tel: +1 207 775 9090

www.condenastjohansens.com/portlandharbor

U.S.A. - FLORIDA (FORT LAUDERDALE)

The Pillars Hotel

111 North Birch Road, Fort Lauderdale, Florida 33304

Tel: +1 954 467 9639

www.condenastjohansens.com/pillarshotel

U.S.A. - MASSACHUSETTS (BOSTON)

Boston Harbor Hotel

70 Rowes Wharf, Boston, Massachusetts 02110

Tel: +1 617 439 7000

www.condenastjohansens.com/bhh

U.S.A. - FLORIDA (MIAMI BEACH)

The Betsy

1440 Ocean Drive, Miami Beach, Florida 33139

Tel: +1 305 531 6100

www.condenastjohansens.com/thebetsyhotel

U.S.A. - MASSACHUSETTS (BOSTON)

Fifteen Beacon

15 Beacon Street, Boston, Massachusetts 02108

Tel: +1 617 670 1500

www.condenastjohansens.com/xvbeacon

Properties listed below can be found in our Recommended Hotels, Inns, Resorts & Spas – The Americas, Atlantic, Caribbean & Pacific 2012 Guide

U.S.A. - MASSACHUSETTS (BOSTON)

Hotel Commonwealth

500 Commonwealth Avenue, Boston,
Massachusetts 02215

Tel: +1 617 933 5000
www.condenastjohansens.com/commonwealth

U.S.A. - NEW YORK (NEW YORK CITY)

Hôtel Plaza Athénée

37 East 64th Street, New York City, New York 10065

Tel: +1 212 734 9100
www.condenastjohansens.com/athenee

U.S.A. - MASSACHUSETTS (CAMBRIDGE)

The Hotel Veritas

One Remington Street in Harvard Square, Cambridge,
Massachusetts 02138

Tel: +1 617 520 5000
www.condenastjohansens.com/thehotelveritas

U.S.A. - NEW YORK (NEW YORK CITY)

The Inn at Irving Place

56 Irving Place, New York, New York City 10003

Tel: +1 212 533 4600
www.condenastjohansens.com/irving

U.S.A. - MASSACHUSETTS (IPSWICH)

The Inn at Castle Hill

280 Argilla Road, Ipswich, Massachusetts 01938

Tel: +1 978 412 2555
www.condenastjohansens.com/castlehill

U.S.A. - NEW YORK (NEW YORK CITY)

The Mark

Madison Avenue at East 77th Street, New York City,
New York 10075

Tel: +1 212 744 4300
www.condenastjohansens.com/themark

U.S.A. - MASSACHUSETTS (LENOX)

Blantyre

16 Blantyre Road, P.O. Box 995, Lenox,
Massachusetts 01240

Tel: +1 413 637 3556
www.condenastjohansens.com/blantyre

U.S.A. - NEW YORK (VERONA)

The Lodge at Turning Stone

5218 Patrick Road, Verona, New York 13478

Tel: +1 315 361 8525
www.condenastjohansens.com/turningstone

U.S.A. - MASSACHUSETTS (MARTHA'S VINEYARD)

The Charlotte Inn

27 South Summer Street, Edgartown, Massachusetts
02539

Tel: +1 508 627 4751/4151
www.condenastjohansens.com/charlotte

U.S.A. - NEW YORK/LONG ISLAND (EAST HAMPTON)

The Baker House 1650

181 Main Street, East Hampton, New York 11937

Tel: +1 631 324 4081
www.condenastjohansens.com/bakerhouse

U.S.A. - MONTANA (DARBY)

Triple Creek Ranch

5551 West Fork Road, Darby, Montana 59829

Tel: +1 406 821 4600
www.condenastjohansens.com/triplecreek

U.S.A. - NEW YORK/LONG ISLAND (SOUTHAMPTON)

1708 House

126 Main Street, Southampton, New York 11968

Tel: +1 631 287 1708
www.condenastjohansens.com/1708house

U.S.A. - NEVADA (LAS VEGAS)

SKYLOFTS at MGM Grand

3977 Las Vegas Boulevard South, Las Vegas,
Nevada 89109

Tel: +1 702 891 3832
www.condenastjohansens.com/skylofts

U.S.A. - NORTH CAROLINA (HIGHLANDS)

Inn at Half Mile Farm

P.O. Box 2769, 214 Half Mile Drive, Highlands,
North Carolina 28741

Tel: +1 828 526 8170
www.condenastjohansens.com/halfmilefarm

U.S.A. - NEW MEXICO (ALBUQUERQUE)

Los Poblanos Inn & Organic Farm

4803 Rio Grande Blvd NW, Los Ranchos de
Albuquerque, New Mexico 87107

Tel: +505 344 9297
www.condenastjohansens.com/lospoblanos

U.S.A. - NORTH CAROLINA (SOUTHERN PINES)

The Jefferson Inn

150 West New Hampshire Avenue, Southern Pines,
North Carolina 28387

Tel: +1 910 692 9911
www.condenastjohansens.com/jeffersoninn

Hotels - The Americas

Properties listed below can be found in our Recommended Hotels, Inns, Resorts & Spas – The Americas, Atlantic, Caribbean & Pacific 2012 Guide

U.S.A. - RHODE ISLAND (NEWPORT)

Castle Hill Inn

590 Ocean Drive, Newport, Rhode Island 02840

Tel: +1 401 849 3800
www.condenastjohansens.com/castlehillinn

U.S.A. - WASHINGTON (SPOKANE)

Hotel Lusso

808 West Sprague Avenue, Spokane, Washington 99201

Tel: +1 509 747 9750
www.condenastjohansens.com/hotellusso

U.S.A. - RHODE ISLAND (NEWPORT)

Vanderbilt Grace

41 Mary Street, Newport, Rhode Island 02840

Tel: +1 401 846 6200
www.condenastjohansens.com/vanderbiltgrace

U.S.A. - WYOMING (JACKSON HOLE)

Amangani

1535 North East Butte Road, P.O. Box 15030, Jackson Hole, Wyoming 83002

Tel: +1 307 734 7333
www.condenastjohansens.com/amangani

U.S.A. - SOUTH CAROLINA (CHARLESTON)

Charleston Harbor Resort & Marina

20 Patriots Point Road, Charleston, South Carolina 29464

Tel: +1 843 856 0028
www.condenastjohansens.com/charlestonharbor

U.S.A. - WYOMING (SARATOGA)

The Lodge and Spa at Brush Creek Ranch

66 Brush Creek Ranch Road, Saratoga, Wyoming 82331

Tel: +1 307 327 5284
www.condenastjohansens.com/brushcreekranch

U.S.A. - VERMONT (WEST TOWNSHEND)

Windham Hill Inn

311 Lawrence Drive, West Townshend, Vermont 05359

Tel: +1 802 874 4080
www.condenastjohansens.com/windhamhillinn

BELIZE - AMBERGRIS CAYE (CAYO ESPANTO)

Cayo Espanto a private island

Ambergris Caye, Cayo Espanto

Tel: +910 323 8355
www.condenastjohansens.com/cayoespanto

U.S.A. - VIRGINIA (MIDDLEBURG)

The Goodstone Inn & Estate

36205 Snake Hill Road, Middleburg, Virginia 20117

Tel: +1 540 687 4645
www.condenastjohansens.com/goodstoneinn

BELIZE - AMBERGRIS CAYE (SAN PEDRO)

Belizean Cove Estates

P.O. Box 1, San Pedro, Ambergris Caye

Tel: +501 226 4741
www.condenastjohansens.com/belizeancove

U.S.A. - VIRGINIA (RICHMOND)

The Jefferson

101 West Franklin Street, Richmond, Virginia 23220

Tel: +1 804 788 8000
www.condenastjohansens.com/jeffersonva

BELIZE - AMBERGRIS CAYE (SAN PEDRO)

Coco Beach Resort

P.O. Box 1, San Pedro, Ambergris Caye

Tel: +501 226 4741
www.condenastjohansens.com/cocobeachbelize

U.S.A. - WASHINGTON (BELLEVUE)

Hotel Bellevue

11200 S.E. 6th Street, Bellevue, Washington 98004

Tel: +1 425 454 4424
www.condenastjohansens.com/bellevue

BELIZE - AMBERGRIS CAYE (NEAR SAN PEDRO)

Matachica Resort & Spa

5 miles North of San Pedro, Ambergris Caye

Tel: +501 226 5010
www.condenastjohansens.com/matachica

U.S.A. - WASHINGTON (SPOKANE)

The Davenport Hotel and Tower

10 South Post Street, Spokane, Washington 99201

Tel: +1 509 455 8888
www.condenastjohansens.com/davenport

BELIZE - AMBERGRIS CAYE (SAN PEDRO)

Victoria House

P.O. Box 22, San Pedro, Ambergris Caye

Tel: +501 226 2067
www.condenastjohansens.com/victoriahouse

Properties listed below can be found in our Recommended Hotels, Inns, Resorts & Spas – The Americas, Atlantic, Caribbean & Pacific 2012 Guide

BELIZE - CAYO DISTRICT (MOUNTAIN PINE RIDGE FOREST RESERVE)

Blancaneaux Lodge

Mountain Pine Ridge Forest Reserve, Cayo District

Tel: +501 824 4912/4914

www.condenastjohansens.com/blancaneaux

BELIZE - CAYO DISTRICT (MOUNTAIN PINE RIDGE FOREST RESERVE)

Hidden Valley Inn

P.O. Box 170, Belmopan

Tel: +501 822 3320

www.condenastjohansens.com/hiddenvalleyinn

BELIZE - CAYO DISTRICT (SAN IGNACIO)

The Lodge at Chaa Creek

P.O. Box 53, San Ignacio, Cayo District

Tel: +501 824 2037

www.condenastjohansens.com/chaacreek

BELIZE - ORANGE WALK DISTRICT (GALLON JUG ESTATE)

Chan Chich Lodge

Gallon Jug Estate, Orange Walk District

Tel: +501 223 4419

www.condenastjohansens.com/chanchich

BELIZE - STANN CREEK DISTRICT (PLACENCIA VILLAGE)

Turtle Inn

Placencia Village, Stann Creek District

Tel: +501 824 4912/4914

www.condenastjohansens.com/turtleinn

BELIZE - TOLEDO DISTRICT (PUNTA GORDA)

Machaca Hill Rainforest Canopy Lodge

P.O. Box 135, Punta Gorda, Toledo District

Tel: +501 722 0050

www.condenastjohansens.com/machacahill

COSTA RICA - ALAJUELA (LA FORTUNA DE SAN CARLOS)

Nayara Hotel, Spa & Gardens

600 Metros Noreste, La Fortuna de San Carlos, Arenal Volcano National Park 33021

Tel: +506 2479 1600

www.condenastjohansens.com/arenalnayara

COSTA RICA - ALAJUELA (LA FORTUNA DE SAN CARLOS)

Tabacón Grand Spa Thermal Resort

La Fortuna de San Carlos, Arenal

Tel: +506 2519 1900

www.condenastjohansens.com/tabacon

COSTA RICA - GUANACASTE (NICOYA)

Hotel Punta Islita

Islita, Nicoya, Guanacaste

Tel: +506 2656 3036

www.condenastjohansens.com/hotelpuntaislita

COSTA RICA - GUANACASTE (PINILLA)

La Posada Hotel

Hacienda Pinilla, Pinilla, Guanacaste

Tel: +506 2680 3000

www.condenastjohansens.com/laposadapinilla

COSTA RICA - LIMÓN (PUERTO VIEJO)

Le Caméléon

Cocles Beach, Puerto Viejo, Limón

Tel: +506 2291 7750

www.condenastjohansens.com/lecameleon

COSTA RICA - PUNTARENAS (MANUEL ANTONIO)

Gaia Hotel & Reserve

Km 2.7 Carretera Quepos, Manuel Antonio, Puntarenas

Tel: +506 2777 9797

www.condenastjohansens.com/gaiahr

COSTA RICA - PUNTARENAS (MANUEL ANTONIO)

The Suu Manuel Antonio

Carretera a Punta Quepos, Manuel Antonio, Puntarenas

Tel: +506 2777 7373

www.condenastjohansens.com/manuelantonio

COSTA RICA - PUNTARENAS (PLAYA DOMINICAL)

Villa Paraiso

Playa Dominical, Puntarenas

Tel: +506 2787 0258

www.condenastjohansens.com/villaparaiso

COSTA RICA - PUNTARENAS (SANTA TERESA)

Florblanca

Santa Teresa, Puntarenas

Tel: +506 2640 0232

www.condenastjohansens.com/florblanca

GUATEMALA - SACATEPÉQUEZ (LA ANTIGUA GUATEMALA)

Casa Quinta Hotel Boutique

5 Av. Sur No. 45, La Antigua Guatemala, Sacatepéquez

Tel: +502 7832 6181/6083

www.condenastjohansens.com/hotelcasaquinta

Hotels - The Americas

Properties listed below can be found in our Recommended Hotels, Inns, Resorts & Spas – The Americas, Atlantic, Caribbean & Pacific 2012 Guide

GUATEMALA - SACATEPÉQUEZ (LA ANTIGUA GUATEMALA)

El Convento Boutique Hotel Antigua Guatemala

2a Avenue Norte 11, La Antigua Guatemala, Sacatepéquez

Tel: +502 7720 7272

www.condenastjohansens.com/elconventoantigua

GUATEMALA - SACATEPÉQUEZ (LA ANTIGUA GUATEMALA)

Palacio de Doña Leonor Antigua Guatemala

4a Calle Oriente Casa No. 8, La Antigua Guatemala, Sacatepéquez 03001

Tel: +502 7832 2281

www.condenastjohansens.com/palaciodeleonor

GUATEMALA - SACATEPÉQUEZ (SAN JUAN ALOTENANGO - LA ANTIGUA GUATEMALA)

La Reunión Antigua Golf Resort

Km. 91.5 Ruta Nacional 14, San Juan Alotenango, Sacatepéquez

Tel: +502 7873 1400

www.condenastjohansens.com/lareunion

GUATEMALA - SOLOLÁ (LAKE ATITLÁN)

Hotel Atitlán

Finca San Buenaventura, Panajachel, Lake Atitlán, Sololá 07010

Tel: +502 7762 1441/2060

www.condenastjohansens.com/hotelatitlan

HONDURAS - BAY ISLANDS (ROATÁN)

Mayoka Lodge

Sandy Bay, Roatán, Bay Islands

Tel: +504 2445 3043

www.condenastjohansens.com/mayokalodge

ARGENTINA - BUENOS AIRES (CIUDAD DE BUENOS AIRES)

Duque Hotel Boutique & Spa

Guatemala 4364, Ciudad de Buenos Aires, Buenos Aires

Tel: +54 11 4832 0312

www.condenastjohansens.com/duquehotel

ARGENTINA - BUENOS AIRES (CIUDAD DE BUENOS AIRES)

Fierro Hotel

Soler 5862, Palermo Hollywood, C1425BYK Ciudad de Buenos Aires, Buenos Aires

Tel: +54 11 3220 6800

www.condenastjohansens.com/fierrohotel

ARGENTINA - BUENOS AIRES (CIUDAD DE BUENOS AIRES)

Legado Mitico

Gurruchaga 1848, C1414DIL Ciudad de Buenos Aires, Buenos Aires

Tel: +54 11 4833 1300

www.condenastjohansens.com/legadomitico

ARGENTINA - BUENOS AIRES (CIUDAD DE BUENOS AIRES)

Mine Hotel Boutique

Gorriti 4770, Palermo Soho, C1414BJL Ciudad de Buenos Aires, Buenos Aires

Tel: +54 11 4832 1100

www.condenastjohansens.com/minehotel

ARGENTINA - RÍO NEGRO (PATAGONIA - SAN CARLOS DE BARILOCHE)

Llao Llao Hotel & Resort, Golf-Spa

Av. Ezequiel Bustillo Km 25, San Carlos de Bariloche, Río Negro, Patagonia

Tel: +54 2944 44 8530

www.condenastjohansens.com/llaollao

BRAZIL - ALAGOAS (BARRA DE SÃO MIGUEL)

Kenoa - Exclusive Beach Spa & Resort

Rua Escritor Jorge Lima 58, Barra de São Miguel, Alagoas 57180-000

Tel: +55 82 3272 1285

www.condenastjohansens.com/kenoaresort

BRAZIL - ALAGOAS (PORTO DE PEDRAS)

Pousada Patacho

Praia do Patacho s/n, Porto de Pedras, Alagoas 57945-000

Tel: +55 82 3298 1253

www.condenastjohansens.com/pousadapatacho

BRAZIL - ALAGOAS (SÃO MIGUEL DOS MILAGRES)

Pousada do Toque

Rua Felisberto de Ataíde, Povoado do Toque, São Miguel dos Milagres, Alagoas 57940-000

Tel: +55 82 3295 1127

www.condenastjohansens.com/pousadadotoque

BRAZIL - BAHIA (ARRAIAL D'AJUDA)

Maitei Hotel

Estrada do Mucugê 475, Arraial D'Ajuda, Porto Seguro, Bahia 45816-000

Tel: +55 73 3575 3877/3799

www.condenastjohansens.com/maitei

BRAZIL - BAHIA (CORUMBAU)

Fazenda São Francisco

Ponta do Corumbau, Bahia

Tel: +55 11 3078 4411

www.condenastjohansens.com/fazenda

BRAZIL - BAHIA (CORUMBAU)

Vila Naiá - Paralelo 17º

Ponta do Corumbau, Bahia

Tel: +55 11 3061 1872

www.condenastjohansens.com/vilanaia

Properties listed below can be found in our Recommended Hotels, Inns, Resorts & Spas – The Americas, Atlantic, Caribbean & Pacific 2012 Guide

BRAZIL - BAHIA (ITACARÉ)

Txai Resort

Rod. Ilhéus-Itacaré km. 48, Itacaré, Bahia 45530-000

Tel: +55 73 2101 5000
www.condenastjohansens.com/txairesort

BRAZIL - PERNAMBUCO (FERNANDO DE NORONHA)

Pousada Maravilha

Rodovia BR-363, s/n, Sueste, Ilha de Fernando de Noronha, Pernambuco 53990-000

Tel: +55 81 3619 0028/1290/0163
www.condenastjohansens.com/maravilha

BRAZIL - BAHIA (PENÍNSULA DE MARAÚ - MARAÚ)

Kiaroa Eco-Luxury Resort

Loteamento da Costa, área SD6, Distrito de Barra Grande, Município de Maraú, Bahia, CEP 45 520-000

Tel: +55 73 3258 6214
www.condenastjohansens.com/kiaroa

BRAZIL - PERNAMBUCO (PORTO DE GALINHAS)

Nannai Beach Resort

Rodovia PE-09, acesso à Muro Alto, Km 3, Ipojuca, Pernambuco 55590-000

Tel: +55 81 3552 0100
www.condenastjohansens.com/nannaibeach

BRAZIL - BAHIA (TRANCOSO)

Etnia Pousada and Boutique

Trancoso, Bahia 45818-000

Tel: + 55 73 3668 1137
www.condenastjohansens.com/etnia

BRAZIL - RIO DE JANEIRO (ARMAÇÃO DOS BÚZIOS)

Villa Rasa Marina

Av. José Bento Ribeiro Dantas 299, Armação dos Búzios, Rio de Janeiro 28950-000

Tel: +55 22 2623 8345
www.condenastjohansens.com/villarasamarina

BRAZIL - BAHIA (TRANCOSO)

Uxua Casa Hotel

Praça São João, Quadrado, Trancoso, Porto Seguro, Bahia 45818-000

Tel: +55 73 3668 2277/2166
www.condenastjohansens.com/uxua

BRAZIL - RIO DE JANEIRO (BÚZIOS)

Casas Brancas Boutique-Hotel & Spa

Alto do Humaitá 10, Armação dos Búzios, Rio de Janeiro 28950-000

Tel: +55 22 2623 1458/1603
www.condenastjohansens.com/casasbrancas

BRAZIL - CEARÁ (JERICOACOARA)

Vila Kalango

Rua das Dunas 30, Jericoacoara, Ceará 62598-000

Tel: +55 88 3669 2290/2289
www.condenastjohansens.com/vilakalango

BRAZIL - RIO DE JANEIRO (BÚZIOS)

Hotel Le Relais La Borie

1374 Rua dos Gravatás, Praia de Geribá, Armação dos Búzios, Rio de Janeiro 28950-000

Tel: +55 22 2620 8504
www.condenastjohansens.com/laborie

BRAZIL - MINAS GERAIS (LIMA DUARTE)

Reserva do Ibitipoca

Fazenda do Engenho, s/n Conceição do Ibitipoca, Lima Duarte, Minas Gerais 36140-000

Tel: +55 32 3281 8174
www.condenastjohansens.com/reservadoibitipoca

BRAZIL - RIO DE JANEIRO (BÚZIOS)

Insólito Boutique Hotel

Rua E1 - Lotes 3 and 4 , Condomínio Atlântico, Armação de Búzios, Rio de Janeiro 28.950-000

Tel: +55 22 2623 2172
www.condenastjohansens.com/insolitohotel

BRAZIL - MINAS GERAIS (TIRADENTES)

Solar da Ponte

Praça das Mercês S/N, Tiradentes, Minas Gerais 36325-000

Tel: +55 32 33 55 12 55
www.condenastjohansens.com/solardaponte

BRAZIL - RIO DE JANEIRO (PARATY)

Casa Turquesa

50 rua Doutor Pereira, Centro Histórico Paraty, Rio de Janeiro

Tel: +55 24 3371 1037/1125
www.condenastjohansens.com/casaturquesa

BRAZIL - PARANÁ (FOZ DO IGUAÇU)

Hotel das Cataratas

Rodovia BR. 469 KM. 32, Iguassu National Park, Foz do Iguaçu, Paraná 85853-000

Tel: +55 45 2102 7000
www.condenastjohansens.com/hoteldascataratas

BRAZIL - RIO DE JANEIRO (PETRÓPOLIS)

Solar do Império

Koeler Avenue, 376 Centro, Petrópolis, Rio de Janeiro

Tel: +55 24 2103 3000
www.condenastjohansens.com/solardoimperio

Hotels - The Americas

Properties listed below can be found in our Recommended Hotels, Inns, Resorts & Spas – The Americas, Atlantic, Caribbean & Pacific 2012 Guide

BRAZIL - RIO DE JANEIRO (PETRÓPOLIS)

Tankamana EcoResort

Estrada Júlio Cápua, S/N Vale Do Cuiabá, Itaipava -
Petrópolis, Rio De Janeiro 25745-050

Tel: +55 24 2232 2900
www.condenastjohansens.com/tankamana

BRAZIL - RIO DE JANEIRO (RIO DE JANEIRO)

Hotel Marina All Suites

Av. Delfim Moreira, 696, Praia do Leblon,
Rio de Janeiro 22441-000

Tel: +55 21 2172 1001
www.condenastjohansens.com/marinaallsuites

BRAZIL - RIO GRANDE DO NORTE (PRAIA DA PIPA)

Toca da Coruja

Avenida Baia dos Golfinhos, 464, Praia da Pipa, Tibau
do Sul, Rio Grande do Norte 59178-000

Tel: +55 84 3246 2226/2225/2121
www.condenastjohansens.com/tocadacoruja

BRAZIL - RIO GRANDE DO SUL (GRAMADO)

Estalagem St. Hubertus

Rua Carrieri, 974, Gramado,
Rio Grande do Sul 95670-000

Tel: +55 54 3286 1273
www.condenastjohansens.com/sthubertus

BRAZIL - RIO GRANDE DO SUL (GRAMADO)

Kurotel Medical Longevity Center and Spa

Rua Nacões Unidas 533, P.O. Box 65, Gramado,
Rio Grande do Sul 95670-000

Tel: +55 54 3295 9393
www.condenastjohansens.com/kurotel

BRAZIL - RIO GRANDE DO SUL (GRAMADO)

La Hacienda Inn and Restaurant

Estrada da Serra Grande 4200, Gramado, Rio Grande
do Sul 95670-000

Tel: +55 54 3295 3025/3088
www.condenastjohansens.com/lahacienda

BRAZIL - RIO GRANDE DO SUL (GRAMADO)

Varanda das Bromélias Boutique Hotel

Rua Alarich Schulz, 198 Bairro Planalto, 95670-000
Gramado, Rio Grande do Sul

Tel: +55 54 3286 0547
www.condenastjohansens.com/varandadasbromelias

BRAZIL - SANTA CATARINA (GOVERNADOR CELSO RAMOS)

Ponta dos Ganchos

Rua Eupídio Alves do Nascimento, 104, Governador
Celso Ramos, Santa Catarina 88190-000

Tel: +55 48 3953 7000
www.condenastjohansens.com/pontadosganchos

BRAZIL - SANTA CATARINA (PRAIA DO ROSA)

Pousada Solar Mirador

Estrada Geral do Rosa s/n, Praia do Rosa, Imbituba,
Santa Catarina 88780-000

Tel: +55 48 3355 6144/6004/6697
www.condenastjohansens.com/solarmirador

BRAZIL - SÃO PAULO (CAMPOS DO JORDÃO)

Hotel Frontenac

Av. Dr. Paulo Ribas, 295 Capivari, Campos do Jordão -
São Paulo 12460-000

Tel: +55 12 3669 1000
www.condenastjohansens.com/frontenac

BRAZIL - SÃO PAULO (ILHABELA)

DPNY Beach Hotel

Av. José Pacheco do Nascimento, 7668, Praia do Curral,
Ilhabela, São Paulo 11630-000

Tel: +55 12 3894 3000
www.condenastjohansens.com/dpnybeach

BRAZIL - SÃO PAULO (SANTO ANTÔNIO DO PINHAL)

Pousada Quinta dos Pinhais

Estrada do Pico Agudo, KM. 3, Santo Antônio do Pinhal,
São Paulo 12450-000

Tel: +55 12 3666 2030/2463/1731
www.condenastjohansens.com/quintadospinhais

BRAZIL - SÃO PAULO (SÃO PAULO)

Hotel Unique

Avenida Brigadeiro Luis Antonio, 4.700 São Paulo,
São Paulo 01402-002

Tel: +55 11 3055 4710/4700
www.condenastjohansens.com/hotelunique

BRAZIL - SÃO PAULO (SERRA DA CANTAREIRA)

Spa Unique Garden

Estrada Laramara, 3500, Serra da Cantareira,
São Paulo 07600-970

Tel: +55 11 4486 8700
www.condenastjohansens.com/uniquegarden

CHILE - IX REGIÓN DE ARAUCANÍA (VILLARRICA/PUCÓN)

**Villarrica Park Lake, a Luxury Collection
Hotel & Spa**

Camino Villarrica - Pucón Km 13, Villarrica,
IX Región de Araucanía

Tel: +56 45 45 00 00
www.condenastjohansens.com/villarrica

CHILE - X REGIÓN DE LOS LAGOS (PATAGONIA - PUERTO MONTT)

Nomads of the Seas

Puerto Montt, X Región de los Lagos

Tel: +562 414 4600
www.condenastjohansens.com/nomadsoftheseas

Properties listed below can be found in our Recommended Hotels, Inns, Resorts & Spas – The Americas, Atlantic, Caribbean & Pacific 2012 Guide

COLOMBIA - BOGOTÁ (SANTAFE DE BOGOTÁ)

Hotel 101 Park House Suites & Spa

Carrera 21 No. 101-10, Santafe de Bogotá, Bogotá

Tel: +57 1 600 0101

www.condenastjohansens.com/101parkhouse

ECUADOR - GALÁPAGOS ISLANDS (SANTA CRUZ ISLAND)

Royal Palm Hotel - Galápagos

Km. 18 Via Baltra, Santa Cruz Island, Galápagos Islands

Tel: +593 5 252 7408

www.condenastjohansens.com/royalpalmgalapagos

COLOMBIA - BOLÍVAR (CARTAGENA DE INDIAS)

Anandá Hotel Boutique

Calle del Cuartel N. 36-77, Cartagena de Indias, Bolívar

Tel: +57 5 664 4452

www.condenastjohansens.com/anandacartagena

ECUADOR - IMBABURA (ANGOCHAGUA)

Hacienda Zuleta

Angochagua, Imbabura

Tel: +593 6 266 2182

www.condenastjohansens.com/zuleta

COLOMBIA - BOLÍVAR (CARTAGENA DE INDIAS)

Casa Pestagua

Calle Santo Domingo No. 33-63, Cartagena de Indias, Bolívar

Tel: +57 5 664 9510/6286

www.condenastjohansens.com/casapestagua

ECUADOR - IMBABURA (SAN PABLO DEL LAGO)

4 Volcanoes Lodge

Calle Sucre, San Pablo del Lago, Imbabura

Tel: +593 6 291 8488

www.condenastjohansens.com/4volcanoes

COLOMBIA - BOLÍVAR (CARTAGENA DE INDIAS)

Hotel Boutique Bovedas de Santa Clara

Calle del Torno No. 39-29, Barrio San Diego, Cartagena de Indias, Bolívar

Tel: +57 5 650 44 65 Ext

www.condenastjohansens.com/bovedasdesantaclara

ECUADOR - PICHINCHA (QUITO)

Hotel Plaza Grande

Calle García Moreno, N5-16 y Chile, Pichincha, Quito

Tel: +593 2 2528 700

www.condenastjohansens.com/plazagrandequito

COLOMBIA - BOLÍVAR (CARTAGENA DE INDIAS)

Hotel LM

Centro Calle de la Mantilla No. 3-56, Cartagena de Indias, Bolívar

Tel: +57 5 664 9100/9564

www.condenastjohansens.com/hotellm

PERÚ - CUSCO (MACHU PICCHU PUEBLO)

Inkaterra Machu Picchu Pueblo Hotel

Machu Picchu Pueblo, Cusco

Tel: +51 1 610 0400

www.condenastjohansens.com/inkaterra

COLOMBIA - BOLÍVAR (CARTAGENA DE INDIAS)

Hotel San Pedro de Majagua

Isla Grande, Islas del Rosario, Cartagena de Indias, Bolívar

Tel: +57 5 650 44 65 Ext 4069-4009

www.condenastjohansens.com/hotelmajagua

PERÚ - LIMA (LIMA)

Swissôtel Lima

Via Central 150, Centro Empresarial Real, San Isidro, Lima 27

Tel: +511 421 4400

www.condenastjohansens.com/swissotellima

ECUADOR - BAHÍA DE CARÁQUEZ (MANABÍ)

Casa Ceibo Boutique Hotel & Spa

Km. 5, Ave. Sixto Durán Ballén, Manabí, Bahía de Caráquez

Tel: +593 5 2399 399

www.condenastjohansens.com/casaceibo

PERÚ - LIMA (VIÑAK)

Refugios Del Perú - Viñak Reichraming

Av. Emilio Cavenecia 225, Of. 321, San Isidro, Lima 27

Tel: +511 421 7777

www.condenastjohansens.com/refugiosdelperu

ECUADOR - GALÁPAGOS ISLANDS (SANTA CRUZ ISLAND)

Galápagos Safari Camp

Finca Palo Santo, Santa Cruz Island, Galápagos Islands

Tel: +593 9 371 7552

www.condenastjohansens.com/galapagossafaricamp

URUGUAY - MALDONADO (JOSÉ IGNACIO)

Casa Suaya

Ruta 10 Km 185, 5, José Ignacio

Tel: +598 4486 2750

www.condenastjohansens.com/casasuaya

Hotels - The Americas, Atlantic & Caribbean

Properties listed below can be found in our Recommended Hotels, Inns, Resorts & Spas – The Americas, Atlantic, Caribbean & Pacific 2012 Guide

URUGUAY - MALDONADO (PUNTA DEL ESTE)

L'Auberge

Carnoustie y Av. del Agua, Barrio Parque del Golf,
Punta del Este CP20100

Tel: +598 4248 8888

www.condenastjohansens.com/laubergeuruguay

URUGUAY - MONTEVIDEO (MONTEVIDEO)

Don Boutique Hotel

Piedras 234, Montevideo, Montevideo

Tel: +598 2915 9999

www.condenastjohansens.com/donhotel

VENEZUELA - PARQUE NACIONAL ARCHIPIÉLAGO LOS ROQUES
(LOS ROQUES)

Posada Acuarela

Calle Las Flores 87, Parque Nacional Archipiélago Los
Roques, Los Roques

Tel: +58 212 953 4235

www.condenastjohansens.com/posadaacuarela

ATLANTIC - BERMUDA (HAMILTON)

Rosedon Hotel

P.O. Box Hm 290, Hamilton Hmax

Tel: +1 441 295 1640

www.condenastjohansens.com/rosedonhotel

CARIBBEAN - ANGUILLA (LITTLE BAY)

Àni Villas

Little Bay

Tel: +1 264 497 7888

www.condenastjohansens.com/anivillas

CARIBBEAN - ANGUILLA (MAUNDAYS BAY)

Cap Juluca

Maundays Bay, Al-2640

Tel: +1 264 497 6666

www.condenastjohansens.com/capjuluca

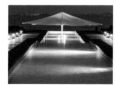

CARIBBEAN - ANGUILLA (RENDEZVOUS BAY)

CuisinArt Golf Resort & Spa

P.O. Box 2000, Rendezvous Bay

Tel: +1 264 498 2000

www.condenastjohansens.com/cuisinartresort

CARIBBEAN - ANGUILLA (SANDY HILL BAY BEACH)

Bird of Paradise

Sandy Hill Bay Beach

Tel: +1 414 791 9461

www.condenastjohansens.com/birdofparadise

CARIBBEAN - ANGUILLA (WEST END)

Sheriva Luxury Villas & Suites

Maundays Bay Road, West End Al-2640

Tel: +1 264 498 9898

www.condenastjohansens.com/sheriva

CARIBBEAN - ANTIGUA (ST. JOHN'S)

Blue Waters

P.O. Box 257, St. John's

Tel: +44 870 360 1245

www.condenastjohansens.com/bluewaters

CARIBBEAN - ANTIGUA (ST. JOHN'S)

Curtain Bluff

P.O. Box 288, St. John's

Tel: +1 268 462 8400

www.condenastjohansens.com/curtainbluff

CARIBBEAN - ANTIGUA (ST. JOHN'S)

Galley Bay Resort & Spa

Five Islands, St. John's

Tel: +1 954 481 8787

www.condenastjohansens.com/galleybay

CARIBBEAN - ANTIGUA (ST. JOHN'S)

The Inn at English Harbour

P.O. Box 187, St. John's

Tel: +1 268 460 1014

www.condenastjohansens.com/innatenglishharbour

CARIBBEAN - BARBADOS (CHRIST CHURCH)

Little Arches

Enterprise Beach Road, Christ Church

Tel: +1 246 420 4689

www.condenastjohansens.com/littlearches

CARIBBEAN - BRITISH VIRGIN ISLANDS (PETER ISLAND)

Peter Island Resort and Spa

Peter Island

Tel: +616 458 6767

www.condenastjohansens.com/peterislandresort

CARIBBEAN - BRITISH VIRGIN ISLANDS (PETER ISLAND)

The Villas at Peter Island

Peter Island

Tel: +616 458 6767

www.condenastjohansens.com/villaspeterisland

Properties listed below can be found in our Recommended Hotels, Inns, Resorts & Spas – The Americas, Atlantic, Caribbean & Pacific 2012 Guide

CARIBBEAN - BRITISH VIRGIN ISLANDS (VIRGIN GORDA)

Biras Creek Resort

North Sound, Virgin Gorda

Tel: +1 248 364 2421

www.condenastjohansens.com/birascreek

CARIBBEAN - SAINT-BARTHÉLEMY (ANSE DE TOINY)

Hôtel Le Toiny

Anse de Toiny

Tel: +590 590 27 88 88

www.condenastjohansens.com/letoiny

CARIBBEAN - CAYMAN ISLANDS (GRAND CAYMAN)

Cotton Tree

375 Conch Point Road, P.O. Box 31324,
Grand Cayman KY1-1206

Tel: +1 345 943 0700

www.condenastjohansens.com/caymancottontree

CARIBBEAN - SAINT-BARTHÉLEMY (GRAND CUL DE SAC)

Hotel Guanahani & Spa

Grand Cul de Sac

Tel: +590 590 27 66 60

www.condenastjohansens.com/guanahani

CARIBBEAN - DOMINICAN REPUBLIC (PUERTO PLATA)

Casa Colonial Beach & Spa

P.O. Box 22, Puerto Plata

Tel: +1 809 320 3232

www.condenastjohansens.com/casacolonial

CARIBBEAN - SAINT-MARTIN (BAIE LONGUE)

La Samanna

P.O. Box 4077, 97064 CEDEX

Tel: +590 590 87 64 00

www.condenastjohansens.com/lasamanna

CARIBBEAN - GRENADA (ST. GEORGE'S)

Azzurra Castle

St. George's

Tel: +1 473 439 0000/9900

www.condenastjohansens.com/azzurracastle

CARIBBEAN - ST. LUCIA (CAP ESTATE)

Cap Maison Resort & Spa

Smugglers Cove Drive, Cap Estate, Gros Islet

Tel: +1 758 457 8670

www.condenastjohansens.com/capmaison

CARIBBEAN - GRENADA (ST. GEORGE'S)

LaSource

Pink Gin Beach, St. George's

Tel: +1 473 444 2556

www.condenastjohansens.com/lasource

CARIBBEAN - ST. LUCIA (SOUFRIÈRE)

Anse Chastanet

Soufrière

Tel: +1 758 459 7000/6100

www.condenastjohansens.com/ansechastanet

CARIBBEAN - GRENADA (ST. GEORGE'S)

Spice Island Beach Resort

Grand Anse Beach, St. George's

Tel: +1 473 444 4258/4423

www.condenastjohansens.com/spiceisland

CARIBBEAN - ST. LUCIA (SOUFRIÈRE)

The Hotel Chocolat

The Rabot Estate, P.O. Box 312, Soufrière

Tel: +44 844 544 1272

www.condenastjohansens.com/hotelchocolat

CARIBBEAN - JAMAICA (MONTEGO BAY)

The Tryall Club

P.O. Box 1206, Montego Bay

Tel: +1 876 956 5660

www.condenastjohansens.com/tryallclub

CARIBBEAN - ST. LUCIA (SOUFRIÈRE)

Jade Mountain at Anse Chastanet

Soufrière

Tel: +1 758 459 4000/6100

www.condenastjohansens.com/jademountain

CARIBBEAN - JAMAICA (OCHO RIOS)

Sandals Royal Plantation, Ocho Rios

Main Street , P.O. Box 2, Ocho Rios

Tel: +1 876 974 5601

www.condenastjohansens.com/sandalsroyalplantation

CARIBBEAN - ST. LUCIA (SOUFRIÈRE)

Ladera

Soufrière

Tel: +1 866 290 0978

www.condenastjohansens.com/ladera

Hotels - Caribbean & Pacific

Properties listed below can be found in our Recommended Hotels, Inns, Resorts & Spas – The Americas, Atlantic, Caribbean & Pacific 2012 Guide

CARIBBEAN - THE GRENADINES (BEQUIA)

Firefly Plantation

Bequia

Tel: +1 784 458 3414

www.condenastjohansens.com/fireflybequia

CARIBBEAN - TURKS & CAICOS ISLANDS (GRACE BAY BEACH)

The Somerset on Grace Bay

Grace Bay Beach, Princess Drive, Providenciales

Tel: +1 649 946 5900

www.condenastjohansens.com/somersetgracebay

CARIBBEAN - THE GRENADINES (MUSTIQUE ISLAND)

Cotton House

Mustique Island

Tel: +1 784 456 4777

www.condenastjohansens.com/cottonhouse

CARIBBEAN - TURKS & CAICOS ISLANDS (PARROT CAY)

Parrot Cay & COMO Shambhala Retreat

P.O. Box 164, Providenciales

Tel: +1 649 946 7788

www.condenastjohansens.com/parrotcay

CARIBBEAN - THE GRENADINES (MUSTIQUE ISLAND)

Firefly

Mustique Island

Tel: +1 784 488 8414

www.condenastjohansens.com/firefly

CARIBBEAN - TURKS & CAICOS ISLANDS (PROVIDENCIALES)

The West Bay Club

Lower Bight Road, Providenciales

Tel: +1 649 946 8550

www.condenastjohansens.com/thewestbayclub

CARIBBEAN - THE GRENADINES (PALM ISLAND)

Palm Island

Palm Island

Tel: +1 954 481 8787

www.condenastjohansens.com/palmisland

CARIBBEAN - TURKS & CAICOS ISLANDS (WEST GRACE BAY BEACH)

Turks & Caicos Club

West Grace Bay Beach, P.O. Box 687, Providenciales

Tel: +1 649 946 5800

www.condenastjohansens.com/turksandcaicos

CARIBBEAN - TURKS & CAICOS ISLANDS (GRACE BAY BEACH)

Gansevoort Turks + Caicos, a Wymara Resort

Lower Bight Road, Grace Bay Beach, Providenciales

Tel: +1 649 941 7555

www.condenastjohansens.com/gansevoorttc

PACIFIC - FIJI ISLANDS (LABASA)

Nukubati Private Island Great Sea Reef

P.O. Box 1928, Labasa

Tel: +679 603 0919

www.condenastjohansens.com/nukubati

CARIBBEAN - TURKS & CAICOS ISLANDS (GRACE BAY BEACH)

Grace Bay Club

Grace Bay Beach, P.O. Box 128, Providenciales

Tel: +1 649 946 5050

www.condenastjohansens.com/gracebayclub

PACIFIC - FIJI ISLANDS (NADI)

The Fiji Orchid

Saweni Beach Road, Lautoka, Nadi

Tel: +679 664 0099

www.condenastjohansens.com/fijiorchid

CARIBBEAN - TURKS & CAICOS ISLANDS (GRACE BAY BEACH)

Point Grace

Grace Bay Beach, P.O. Box 700, Providenciales

Tel: +1 649 946 5096

www.condenastjohansens.com/pointgrace

PACIFIC - FIJI ISLANDS (QAMEA ISLAND)

Qamea Resort & Spa

P.A. Matei, Taveuni

Tel: +649 360 0858

www.condenastjohansens.com/qamea

CARIBBEAN - TURKS & CAICOS ISLANDS (GRACE BAY BEACH)

The Regent Palms, Turks & Caicos

Grace Bay Beach, P.O. Box 681, Providenciales

Tel: +649 946 8666

www.condenastjohansens.com/regentpalms

PACIFIC - FIJI ISLANDS (YASAWA ISLANDS)

Turtle Island, Fiji

Turtle Island, Yasawa Islands

Tel: +1 360 256 4347

www.condenastjohansens.com/turtleisland

Properties listed below can be found in our Recommended Hotels, Inns, Resorts & Spas – The Americas, Atlantic, Caribbean & Pacific 2012 Guide

PACIFIC - VANUATU (EFATE ISLAND)

Eratap Beach Resort

Eratap Point, Port Vila, Efate Island

Tel: +678 554 5007

www.condenastjohansens.com/eratap

PACIFIC - VANUATU (EFATE ISLAND)

The Havannah Vanuatu

Samoa Point, P.O. Box 4, Port Vila, Efate Island

Tel: + 678 551 8060

www.condenastjohansens.com/thehavannah

LIQUID ASSETS

www.hildon.com or ☎ +44 (0) 1794 302747

Index by Property

0-9

41 ....**London** **79**
51 Buckingham Gate, Taj Suites and Residences ..London...97

A

Airds Hotel...Port Appin 135
Alexandra Hotel and Restaurant ....Lyme Regis 64
Armathwaite Hall Country House Hotel and Spa ..Keswick 46
Ashdown Park Hotel and Country Club ....Forest Row 103
Ashford Castle ....Cong 128
The Atlantic Hotel ....Jersey 14

B

Bailiffscourt Hotel & Spa..Arundel 106
Barnsley House ....Cirencester............................68

Beaufort House ....**London** **89**
Bibury Court ....Bibury 67
Budock Vean - The Hotel on the River.....................Falmouth 39
Burleigh Court...Minchinhampton 71

C

Cahernane House Hotel..Killarney 127
Calcot Manor Hotel & Spa ....Tetbury.................................73
Captains Club Hotel & Spa ....Christchurch 61
Carlyon Bay Hotel, Spa & Golf Resort.....................Carlyon Bay 36
Cashel House ....Connemara..........................125
The Castle at Taunton...Taunton..............................100
Castle House ....Hereford................................77
Castlemartyr Resort ....Cork 123
Cheval Calico House ....London..................................82
Cheval Gloucester Park..London..................................85

Cheval Knightsbridge ....**London** **90**
Cheval Phoenix House ....London..................................80
Cheval Thorney Court ....London..................................86
Chewton Glen ....New Forest............................75
Christchurch Harbour Hotel & Spa ....Christchurch 62
The Club Hotel & Spa, Bohemia Restaurant ....Jersey 15
Combe House..Exeter 57
Coworth Park ....Ascot 31
Craigellachie Hotel of Speyside ....Craigellachie 134

D

Dale Head Hall Lakeside Hotel ....Keswick 48
Danesfield House Hotel and Spa ....Marlow-On-Thames................33
Dormy House...Broadway 117
Dromoland Castle..Newmarket-On-Fergus 122
Dukes Hotel ....Bath 28

E

The Egerton House Hotel ....London..................................91

F

Farlam Hall Hotel..Brampton 44
Felbridge Hotel & Spa ....East Grinstead 108
Fischer's Baslow Hall ....Baslow 53
Fota Island Hotel & Spa...Fota Island 124
The French Horn..Reading................................32

Index by Property

G

The g Hotel .... Galway 126
The George Of Stamford .... Stamford 78
Gidleigh Park .... Chagford 56
Gilpin Hotel & Lake House .... Windermere 49
The Grand Hotel .... Eastbourne 102
Gravetye Manor .... West Hoathly 111
Greywalls and Chez Roux .... Muirfield 137
The Grove Hotel .... Narberth 147

H

Hambleton Hall .... Oakham 99
Hampton Manor .... Solihull 113

Hoar Cross Hall Spa Resort .... **Lichfield** **101**
Holbeck Ghyll Country House Hotel .... Windermere 50
Horsted Place Country House Hotel .... Lewes 104
Hotel Riviera .... Sidmouth 59

I

Inver Lodge Hotel and Chez Roux .... Lochinver 140
Inverlochy Castle .... Fort William 138

K

Kensington House Hotel .... London 87
Knockranny House Hotel & Spa .... Westport 129

L

Lake Country House & Spa .... Llangammarch Wells 149
Lake Vyrnwy Hotel & Spa .... Lake Vyrnwy 148
Lakeside Hotel on Lake Windermere .... Windermere 52
Lime Wood .... Lyndhurst 74
Linthwaite House Hotel .... Windermere 51
The Lodore Falls Hotel .... Keswick 47
Longueville Manor .... Jersey 16
Lower Slaughter Manor .... Lower Slaughter 69
Lucknam Park Hotel & Spa .... Bath 115
The Lugger Hotel .... Portloe 41
Luton Hoo Hotel, Golf & Spa .... Luton 29

M

The Mandeville Hotel .... London 92
The Manor House Hotel .... Moreton-in-Marsh 72

The May Fair .... London 93
The Mayflower Hotel .... London 83

The Mere Golf Resort & Spa .... **Knutsford** **35**
Meudon Hotel .... Falmouth 40
Milestone Hotel .... London 88
Moore Place Hotel .... Milton Keynes 30

N

Nailcote Hall .... Coventry 112
The Nare Hotel .... Carne Beach 37
Netherwood Hotel .... Grange-Over-Sands 45
The New Linden Hotel .... London 95
Newick Park .... Lewes 105
Northcote Manor Country House Hotel .... Burrington 55

O

Ockenden Manor .... **Cuckfield** **107**
Otterburn Hall .... Otterburn 98

P

Park House Hotel & PH²O Spa..........................Midhurst.........................109
Penmaenuchaf Hall..Dolgellau........................146
The Priory Hotel...Wareham.........................65

R

Risley Hall Hotel and Spa................................Risley............................54
The Ritz-Carlton, Powerscourt.........................Enniskerry.......................130

Rockliffe Hall ....**Darlington** **66**
Rocpool Reserve and Chez Roux ....Inverness........................139
Rose-In-Vale Country House Hotel....................St Agnes..........................42
Rudding Park Hotel, Spa & Golf.......................Harrogate........................118
Ruthin Castle Hotel...Ruthin...........................145

S

Simonstone Hall ....Hawes............................119
Sofitel London St James..................................London............................96
The Spread Eagle Hotel & Spa.........................Midhurst........................110
St Ives Harbour Hotel - Porthminster ....St Ives............................43
St Michael's Hotel & Spa.................................Falmouth..........................38
St Tudno Hotel & Restaurant...........................Llandudno.......................144
Stoke Park..Stoke Poges.......................34
Stonefield Castle..Tarbert..........................136
Summer Lodge Country House Hotel, Restaurant and Spa.....................
                                                         Evershot..........................63

T

The Tides Reach Hotel.....................................Salcombe..........................58
Twenty Nevern Square ....London............................84
Tylney Hall...Rotherwick........................76

W

Washbourne Court..Lower Slaughter..................70
Watersmeet Hotel..Woolacombe........................60
Welcombe Hotel Spa & Golf Club ....Stratford-Upon-Avon...........114
Westbury Hotel..London............................94
Whatley Manor...Malmesbury.....................116
The Wyndham Grand London Chelsea Harbour. London............................81

Index by Location

London

Buckingham Palace...............41 79
Chelsea ....Cheval Phoenix House 80
Chelsea Harbour.....................The Wyndham Grand London Chelsea Harbour ...81
City ....Cheval Calico House 82
Earls Court ....The Mayflower Hotel........................83
Earls Court ....Twenty Nevern Square......................84
Kensington............................Cheval Gloucester Park....................85
Kensington............................Cheval Thorney Court......................86
Kensington............................Kensington House Hotel...................87
Kensington............................Milestone Hotel.............................88
Knightsbridge.........................Beaufort House.............................89
Knightsbridge.........................Cheval Knightsbridge......................90
Knightsbridge.........................The Egerton House Hotel..................91
Mayfair.................................The Mandeville Hotel......................92
Mayfair.................................The May Fair................................93
Mayfair.................................Westbury Hotel.............................94
Notting Hill............................The New Linden Hotel.....................95
Piccadilly ....Sofitel London St James..................96
Westminster...........................51 Buckingham Gate, Taj Suites and Residences...97

England

A

Arundel.................................Bailiffscourt Hotel & Spa..................106

Ascot...................................**Coworth Park**...........................**31**

B

Barnsley................................Barnsley House.............................68
Barnstaple, Umberleigh ....Northcote Manor Country House Hotel..................55
Baslow..................................Fischer's Baslow Hall.....................53
Bassenthwaite Lake.............Armathwaite Hall Country House Hotel and Spa..46
Bath.....................................Dukes Hotel.................................28
Bath.....................................Lucknam Park Hotel & Spa 115
Berkswell...............................Nailcote Hall...............................112
Bibury..................................Bibury Court................................67
Borrowdale ....The Lodore Falls Hotel....................47
Bowness................................Linthwaite House Hotel....................51

Index by Location

Brampton .... Farlam Hall Hotel 44
Broadway .... Dormy House 117
Burrington .... Northcote Manor Country House Hotel 55

C

Carlyon Bay .... Carlyon Bay Hotel, Spa & Golf Resort 36
Carne Beach .... The Nare Hotel 37

Chagford .... **Gidleigh Park** **56**
Christchurch .... Captains Club Hotel & Spa 61
Christchurch .... Christchurch Harbour Hotel & Spa 62
Cirencester .... Barnsley House 68
Climping .... Bailiffscourt Hotel & Spa 106
Colerne .... Lucknam Park Hotel & Spa 115
Cotswolds .... The Manor House Hotel 72
Coventry .... Nailcote Hall 112
Cuckfield .... Ockenden Manor 107

D

Darlington .... Rockliffe Hall 66
Dorchester .... Summer Lodge Country House Hotel,
                                        Restaurant and Spa 63

E

East Grinstead .... Felbridge Hotel & Spa 108
East Grinstead .... Gravetye Manor 111
Eastbourne .... The Grand Hotel 102
Evershot .... Summer Lodge Country House Hotel,
                                        Restaurant and Spa 63
Exeter .... Combe House 57

F

Falmouth .... Budock Vean - The Hotel on the River 39
Falmouth .... Meudon Hotel 40
Falmouth .... St Michael's Hotel & Spa 38
Felbridge .... Felbridge Hotel & Spa 108
Forest Row .... Ashdown Park Hotel and Country Club 103

G

Gatwick .... Ockenden Manor 107
Grange-Over-Sands .... Netherwood Hotel 45
Gyllyngvase Beach .... St Michael's Hotel & Spa 38

H

Harrogate .... Rudding Park Hotel, Spa & Golf 118
Hawes .... Simonstone Hall 119
Heathrow .... Stoke Park 34
Hereford .... Castle House 77
Hoar Cross .... Hoar Cross Hall Spa Resort 101
Honiton .... Combe House 57
Hurworth-on-Tees .... Rockliffe Hall 66

K

Keswick .... Armathwaite Hall Country House Hotel and Spa ..46
Keswick .... Dale Head Hall Lakeside Hotel 48
Keswick .... The Lodore Falls Hotel 47
Knutsford .... The Mere Golf Resort & Spa 35

L

Lake Thirlmere .... Dale Head Hall Lakeside Hotel 48
Lewes .... Horsted Place Country House Hotel 104
Lewes .... Newick Park 105
Lichfield .... Hoar Cross Hall Spa Resort 101
Little Horsted .... Horsted Place Country House Hotel 104
Lower Slaughter .... Lower Slaughter Manor 69
Lower Slaughter .... Washbourne Court 70
Luton .... Luton Hoo Hotel, Golf & Spa 29
Lyme Regis .... Alexandra Hotel and Restaurant 64
Lyndhurst .... Lime Wood 74

M

Malmesbury .... Whatley Manor 116

Marlow-On-Thames .... **Danesfield House Hotel and Spa** **33**
Mawnan Smith .... Budock Vean - The Hotel on the River 39
Mawnan Smith .... Meudon Hotel 40
Midhurst .... Park House Hotel & PH²O Spa 109
Midhurst .... The Spread Eagle Hotel & Spa 110
Milton Keynes .... Moore Place Hotel 30
Minchinhampton .... Burleigh Court 71
Mithian .... Rose-In-Vale Country House Hotel 42
Moreton-in-Marsh .... The Manor House Hotel 72
Mortehoe .... Watersmeet Hotel 60

N

New Forest ....Chewton Glen...75
Newby Bridge.........................Lakeside Hotel on Lake Windermere.......................52
Newick ....Newick Park... 105

O

Oakham.................................Hambleton Hall..99
Otterburn ....Otterburn Hall...98

P

Portloe ....The Lugger Hotel..41

R

Reading ....The French Horn...32

Risley ....Risley Hall Hotel and Spa 54
Roseland Peninsula ....The Lugger Hotel...41
Rotherwick..............................Tylney Hall...76

S

St Agnes ....Rose-In-Vale Country House Hotel 42
St Ives ....St Ives Harbour Hotel - Porthminster......................43
St Mawes.................................The Nare Hotel..37
Salcombe ....The Tides Reach Hotel..58
Sidmouth ....Hotel Riviera..59
Solihull ....Hampton Manor... 113
Sonning-On-Thames ....The French Horn...32
South Sands ....The Tides Reach Hotel..58
Stamford ....The George Of Stamford...78
Stoke Poges ....Stoke Park...34
Stratford-Upon-Avon ....Welcombe Hotel Spa & Golf Club........................ 114

T

Taunton ....The Castle at Taunton 100
Tetbury ....Calcot Manor Hotel & Spa......................................73

U

Upper Wensleydale ....Simonstone Hall.. 119

W

Wareham ....The Priory Hotel 65
West Hoathly...........................Gravetye Manor 111
Windermere ....Gilpin Hotel & Lake House.......................................49
Windermere ....Holbeck Ghyll Country House Hotel.......................50

Windermere.......................Lakeside Hotel on Lake Windermere...............52
Windermere ....Linthwaite House Hotel..51
Woburn....................................Moore Place Hotel..30
Woolacombe............................Watersmeet Hotel 60

Channel Islands

Jersey.......................................The Atlantic Hotel...14
Jersey.......................................The Club Hotel & Spa, Bohemia Restaurant...........15
Jersey.......................................Longueville Manor..16

Index by Location / Consortium

Ireland

Cong .... Ashford Castle 128
Connemara .... Cashel House 125
Cork .... Castlemartyr Resort 123

Enniskerry .... The Ritz-Carlton, Powerscourt 130
Fota Island .... Fota Island Hotel & Spa 124
Galway .... The g Hotel 126
Killarney .... Cahernane House Hotel 127
Newmarket-On-Fergus .... Dromoland Castle 122
Westport .... Knockranny House Hotel & Spa 129

Scotland

Banffshire .... Craigellachie Hotel of Speyside 134
Craigellachie .... Craigellachie Hotel of Speyside 134
Fort William .... Inverlochy Castle 138
Gullane .... Greywalls and Chez Roux 137
Inverness .... Rocpool Reserve and Chez Roux 139
Lochinver .... Inver Lodge Hotel and Chez Roux 140
Muirfield .... Greywalls and Chez Roux 137
Port Appin .... Airds Hotel 135
Sutherland .... Inver Lodge Hotel and Chez Roux 140
Tarbert .... Stonefield Castle 136

Wales

Dolgellau .... Penmaenuchaf Hall 146
Lake Vyrnwy .... Lake Vyrnwy Hotel & Spa 148
Llandudno .... St Tudno Hotel & Restaurant 144
Llangammarch Wells .... Lake Country House & Spa 149
Narberth .... The Grove Hotel 147
Penmaenpool .... Penmaenuchaf Hall 146
Ruthin .... Ruthin Castle Hotel 145

Index by Consortium

Ireland's Blue Book

Ireland

Cashel House .... Galway 125

Leading Hotels of the World

England

Milestone Hotel .... London 88

Ireland

Ashford Castle .... Mayo 128

Pride of Britain members

England

Luton Hoo Hotel, Golf & Spa .... Bedfordshire 29
The French Horn .... Berkshire 32
The Nare Hotel .... Cornwall 37
Holbeck Ghyll Country House Hotel .... Cumbria 50
Linthwaite House Hotel .... Cumbria 51
The Priory Hotel .... Dorset 65
Calcot Manor Hotel & Spa .... Gloucestershire 73
Tylney Hall .... Hampshire 76
Ashdown Park Hotel and Country Club .... East Sussex 103
Bailiffscourt Hotel & Spa .... West Sussex 106
Ockenden Manor .... West Sussex 107
Dormy House .... Worcestershire 117

Wales

Lake Country House & Spa .... Powys 149

Relais & Châteaux

Channel Islands

Longueville Manor .... Channel Islands 16

England

Farlam Hall Hotel .... Cumbria 44
Gilpin Hotel & Lake House .... Cumbria 49
Gidleigh Park .... Devon 56
Summer Lodge Country House Hotel, Restaurant and Spa ....
                                                     Dorset 63
Lower Slaughter Manor .... Gloucestershire 69
Lime Wood .... Hampshire 74
Chewton Glen .... Hampshire 75
Hambleton Hall .... Rutland 99
Gravetye Manor .... West Sussex 111
Lucknam Park Hotel & Spa .... Wiltshire 115
Whatley Manor .... Wiltshire 116

Scotland

Inverlochy Castle .... Highland 138

Small Luxury Hotels of the World

Channel Islands

The Atlantic Hotel .... Channel Islands 14

England

Luton Hoo Hotel, Golf & Spa .... Bedfordshire 29
Danesfield House Hotel and Spa .... Buckinghamshire 33
Stoke Park .... Buckinghamshire 34
Holbeck Ghyll Country House Hotel .... Cumbria 50
Tylney Hall .... Hampshire 76
The Grand Hotel .... East Sussex 102
Ashdown Park Hotel and Country Club .... East Sussex 103

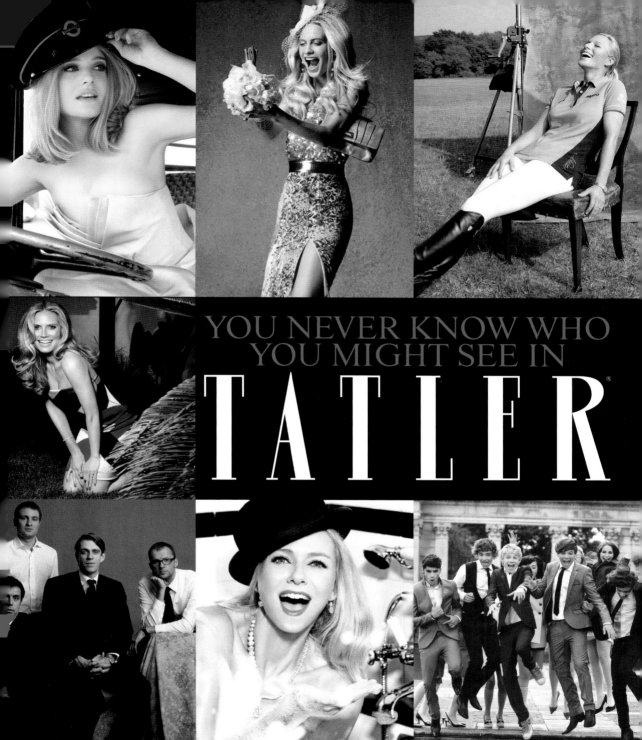

YOU NEVER KNOW WHO
YOU MIGHT SEE IN

TATLER®